YORK NOTES

Much Ado About Nothing

William Shakespeare

Notes by Sarah Rowbotham

203 471

 York Press

Sarah Rowbotham is hereby identified as author of this work in accordance with Section 77 of the Copyright, Designs and Patents Act 1988

YORK PRESS
322 Old Brompton Road, London SW5 9JH

PEARSON EDUCATION LIMITED
Edinburgh Gate, Harlow,
Essex CM20 2JE, United Kingdom
Associated companies, branches and representatives throughout the world

First published 1999
Fourth impression 2004

ISBN 0-582-38193-2

Designed by Vicki Pacey
Illustrated by Sue Scott
Sketch of Globe by Gerry Grace
Phototypeset by Gem Graphics, Trenance, Mawgan Porth, Cornwall
Colour reproduction and film output by Spectrum Colour
Produced by Pearson Education Asia Limited, Hong Kong

Contents

PREFACE

York Notes are designed to give you a broader perspective on works of literature studied at GCSE and equivalent levels. We have carried out extensive research into the needs of the modern literature student prior to publishing this new edition. Our research showed that no existing series fully met students' requirements. Rather than present a single authoritative approach, we have provided alternative viewpoints, empowering students to reach their own interpretations of the text. York Notes provide a close examination of the work and include biographical and historical background, summaries, glossaries, analyses of characters, themes, structure and language, cultural connections and literary terms.

If you look at the Contents page you will see the structure for the series. However, there's no need to read from the beginning to the end as you would with a novel, play, poem or short story. Use the Notes in the way that suits you. Our aim is to help you with your understanding of the work, not to dictate how you should learn.

York Notes are written by English teachers and examiners, with an expert knowledge of the subject. They show you how to succeed in coursework and examination assignments, guiding you through the text and offering practical advice. Questions and comments will extend, test and reinforce your knowledge. Attractive colour design and illustrations improve clarity and understanding, making these Notes easy to use and handy for quick reference.

York Notes are ideal for:
- Essay writing
- Exam preparation
- Class discussion

The author of these Notes is Sarah Rowbotham, who teaches at a comprehensive school in Sheffield. She is a senior examiner in GCSE English for one of the largest examination bodies. In this series she has written the Notes on *Nineteenth Century Short Stories* and *Jane Eyre*.

The text used in these Notes is the Players' Shakespeare edition, edited by J. H. Walter (Heinemann, 1979).

Health Warning: **This study guide will enhance your understanding, but should not replace the reading of the original text and/or study in class.**

PART ONE

INTRODUCTION

HOW TO STUDY A PLAY

You have bought this book because you wanted to study a play on your own. This may supplement classwork.

- Drama is a special 'kind' of writing (the technical term is 'genre') because it needs a performance in the theatre to arrive at a full interpretation of its meaning. When reading a play you have to imagine how it should be performed; the words alone will not be sufficient. Think of gestures and movements.

- Drama is always about conflict of some sort (it may be below the surface). Identify the conflicts in the play and you will be close to identifying the large ideas or themes which bind all the parts together.

- Make careful notes on themes, characters, plot and any subplots of the play.

- Playwrights find nonrealistic ways of allowing an audience to see into the minds and motives of their characters. The 'soliloquy', in which a character speaks directly to the audience, is one such device. Does the play you are studying have any such passages?

- Which characters do you like or dislike in the play? Why? Do your sympathies change as you see more of these characters?

- Think of the playwright writing the play. Why were these particular arrangements of events, these particular sets of characters and these particular speeches chosen?

Studying on your own requires self-discipline and a carefully thought-out work plan in order to be effective. Good luck.

Shakespeare's background

Family history

William Shakespeare was born in Stratford-upon-Avon in Warwickshire, and baptised on 26 April 1564 at Holy Trinity Church. Common agreement places his date of birth three days earlier, making his birthday St George's Day. His father, John Shakespeare, was a successful merchant who began his career trading in leather goods and over the years became an important citizen in the town, eventually rising to the office of High Bailiff, which is similar to the function of mayor.

Many details are vague, as recrods were not kept in the same way they are today.

One of his responsibilities was of Town Constable (the role assigned to Dogberry but presumably not as a slight upon his father's ability!). Shakespeare attended King's New School, a grammar school in Stratford. He had seven brothers and sisters. His father eventually died in 1601, but his mother Mary did not die until 1609. Thus she lived to see how successful her son became.

Education and early works

The grammar school would have endowed Shakespeare with the tools to become a schoolmaster: elementary history, Latin, mathematics and logic. He was married at eighteen to Anne Hathaway, a woman eight years his senior, who was already pregnant with their first daughter. They had twins two years later, and it is around this time that Shakespeare left Stratford for

Shakespeare had practical experience as an actor before writing plays.

London. He is first mentioned in 1592 as being a playwright and actor, and was known to have played roles in two plays by a contemporary and rival Ben Johnson. He is also listed as part of a company of actors called Lord Pembroke's Men, and then with the Lord Chamberlain's Men. It was during this period that some of his early plays were written, among them the comedies *The Taming of the Shrew* and *The Comedy of Errors*.

THE THEATRE

Shakespeare was always playwright and actor first, storyteller second.

By 1599 Shakespeare had become fully integrated into the theatre world of London. He was involved in the establishment of the Globe theatre, for which institution he wrote and performed in several plays with the Lord Chamberlain's Men (who became known as The King's Men after receiving the patronage of James I in 1603). Most of his plays were performed here; the theatre enjoyed fourteen years of dramatic activity before it burned to the ground in 1613.

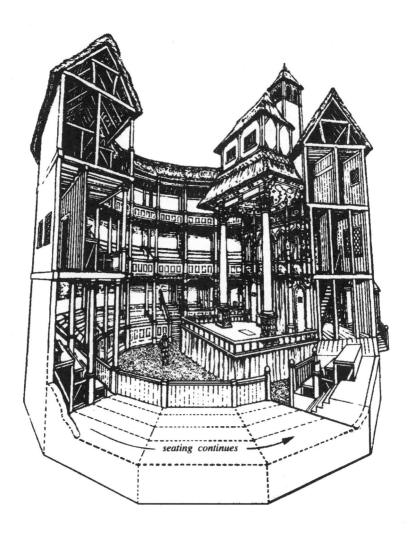

seating continues

THE PLAYWRIGHT

Because dating is so vague, we have to look for accounts of first performances to assess when the plays were written.

Most of Shakespeare's work seems to have been written during his time in London, apart from some of the later 'romances' such as *The Winter's Tale* and *The Tempest*, which were definitely conceived during his last years in Stratford. *Much Ado About Nothing* is a relatively early play; first accounts of its performance at The Globe date it at around 1598. Thus it was probably written shortly after *Romeo and Juliet*, but before the tragedies of *Macbeth*, *Hamlet* and *King Lear*. As a comedy it stands with *Twelfth Night*, *The Merry Wives of Windsor* and *As You Like It*: the group known as the 'mature' comedies.

LATER YEARS

Shakespeare became extremely successful as a playwright. By the late 1590s he had acquired a large house in Stratford and a great deal of land in the area. His house, New House, was home to his retirement to Stratford in 1611. He was lucky enough to enjoy the benefits of his success in his own lifetime. He died on 23 April 1616, the author of thirty-seven plays, several **epic poems** and over 100 **sonnets** (see Literary Terms).

CONTEXT & SETTING

DRAMATIC BACKGROUND

Most of Shakespeare's plays, although original works, utilised plot-lines from other sources, often Italian narrative poems and **novellas** (see Literary Terms). Although the **plot** (see Literary Terms) of Beatrice and Benedick appears to be original, there are several versions of the Claudio and Hero story. The most famous author of these is Edmund Spenser, whose epic narrative poem *The Faerie Queene* (1596) would have most certainly been read by Shakespeare. In Spenser's version, the heroine Claribella (Hero) is killed by her duped lover (Claudio), who then poisons his deceiver Philomen (Don John). Shakespeare evidently decided to lighten the tone of the story considerably in his comic version.

The idea of a pastoral idyll

The term 'pastoral' links to the word 'pasture'; think of green fields, Mother Nature, a simple peaceful life.

Elizabethan theatre often contained more than one fictional world. The idea of a 'pastoral' existence was of a life of peace and harmony, where characters operated in a natural world and concerned themselves with matters of the heart. It was often a place of escape; a safe haven where problems could be resolved before the launch back into the 'real' world. Shakespeare used this idea in many of his comedies: *The Merchant of Venice* has Belmont, *As You Like It* has the Forest of Arden, and *A Midsummer Night's Dream* has the enchanted wood. *Twelfth Night* and *Much Ado About Nothing* are unusual in that all the action takes place away from the world of court, finance and business. Messina's household is untouched by the world. Outside events are referred to, but none of the central characters are directly affected by them. The characters form a miniature society within themselves; there is a recognisable structure and hierarchy among them: with Don Pedro as the highest authority, down to Dogberry, Verges and the Watch as the most menial.

Domesticity

Domestic concerns take precedence over matters of the world throughout this play. Even the 'war' from which the visiting gentlemen return is of a familial nature – hints that Don John had attempted to overthrow Don

Pedro's authority are alluded to by Conrade. From the beginning it is matters of family and the heart which will rule the course of the dramatic action. The successful pairings off of Claudio and Hero and Beatrice and Benedick are the driving forces of the play.

Elizabethans were pragmatists on the subject of marriage. It was a busines/financial contract far more than a romantic liaison.

Nevertheless there is a sense of marriage as a pragmatic business transaction also, especially to those most closely on the periphery of the relationship between Claudio and Hero. Both Leonato and Don Pedro have things to gain from this marriage. However, Shakespeare makes sure that Claudio's motive is love rather than financial gain, to reaffirm the status of the play firmly as **romantic comedy** (see Literary Terms).

PART TWO

SUMMARIES

GENERAL SUMMARY

Act I Leonato, Governor of Messina, receives word that a group of young noblemen led by Don Pedro of Arragon plan to pay his home a visit following recent success at war. Leonato is honoured and delighted at the news, and great preparations ensue for receiving the guests.

Don Pedro brings along his 'bastard' half brother Don John. The two are recently reconciled after a long disagreement. Don John appears to be a sullen, dark-natured individual. A young nobleman Claudio is also of the party. He notices Leonato's daughter Hero and immediately falls in love with her.

Leonato's niece Beatrice enquires after Signor Benedick, another friend of Don Pedro. It appears that the two are acquainted of old, and have nothing but bad to say of each other. They begin quarrelling as soon as they meet.

Claudio tells Benedick and Don Pedro of his love for Hero. Don Pedro promises to help by wooing Hero for Claudio, and thereby securing their marriage. This conversation is overheard by a servant, who mistakenly believes that it is Don Pedro who loves Hero. Leonato's brother Antonio tells Leonato this. The conversation is also overheard by Don John's associate Borachio. Don John is jealous and resentful of Claudio, and vows to do anything to subvert his plans for happiness with Hero.

Act II Don John makes his first attempt to thwart Claudio's plans by circulating a rumour that Don Pedro means to have Hero for himself. This plot is quickly discovered. The second plan is far more sinister, however. Borachio comes up with a scheme to fool Claudio into thinking that Hero is having an affair with another man. He plans to fool Hero's waiting-woman Margaret into dressing up as Hero and playing out a love scene which will be overheard by Claudio and Don Pedro.

At the same time, Don Pedro, Leonato, Claudio and Hero have noticed the suitability and compatibility of Beatrice and Benedick, and engage in a far more lighthearted scheme to bring the two together. They allow Benedick to 'overhear' them discussing Beatrice's love for Benedick. He is shocked and stunned by this, but instantly resolves to return her 'affection'.

Act III   The plotters turn their attention to Beatrice. Hero and Ursula connive to make Beatrice overhear a similar conversation to the one Benedick heard between Don Pedro and Leonato. She is similarly ensnared by the idea that Benedick loves her but will not declare himself for fear of her sarcastic nature and conceit.

Don John's plot for Hero and Claudio begins to take effect. He announces that he has proof of her infidelity and means to show the shocked Claudio and Don Pedro later that day.

The comic characters of Dogberry, Verges and the Watch play out a scene of misconception and misunderstanding, designed to show the inappropriacy of their station as officers of the law. However, they overhear Conrade and Borachio discussing the sinister plot. They recognise villainy when they hear it and arrest the two men. They report the arrest to Leonato, but he is too busy to listen.

Act IV   Claudio chooses to denounce Hero in the most public arena: at their wedding ceremony. Hero protests her innocence but no-one appears to believe her except Beatrice, Benedick and Friar Francis. Hero faints from the shock of their attack upon her integrity. The Friar comes up with a plan: it is decided to feign Hero's death in the hopes that this will make Claudio realise how stupid he has been. Leonato is comforted by the knowledge that if the slander is proved to be true, he will be able to whisk Hero away secretly under cover of her assumed death.

Beatrice and Benedick are now united in their concern for Hero. After openly declaring their feelings for each other, Beatrice commands Benedick to 'kill Claudio' for slandering the honour of her friend. He reluctantly agrees. At the same time, Dogberry and the Watch discover the plot through questioning their prisoners Borachio and Conrade. Don John flees in disgrace, and it is generally announced that Hero has died of shock.

Act V

Leonato and Benedick both challenge Don Pedro and Claudio to recant their accusations. This they refuse to do. When Dogberry and Verges enter with their prisoners, however, they are forced to acknowledge their mistake. Claudio is shocked at the news of Hero's 'death' and promises Leonato that he will do anything to preserve the honour of her memory. Leonato makes him promise to marry his 'niece' instead; this Claudio agrees to do.

At the scene of the wedding, Leonato's 'niece' is unmasked as Hero. Claudio is forgiven, Beatrice and Benedick make a public declaration of their love, and news reaches Messina that Don John is captured and will be punished for his villainy. The play ends with a dance of celebration.

Act I

Scene 1

Claudio and Benedick are given honourable status from the start.

The play opens in the peaceful setting of Messina. Leonato, Governor of Messina, is delivered a letter by a messenger announcing the imminent arrival of Don Pedro, Prince of Arragon. Don Pedro has recently won some kind of military victory. Leonato reads that Don Pedro will be accompanied by his newly reconciled 'bastard' brother Don John, and there are hints later on that the military conflict was between these two. The letter mentions that a young nobleman named Claudio will be accompanying Don Pedro. The Messenger speaks very highly of Claudio, relating descriptions of his bravery and honourable conduct in battle.

Leonato's daughter Hero and niece Beatrice listen avidly to the news. Beatrice questions the Messenger as to whether 'Signor Mountanto' will also be accompanying the party. This confuses the messenger, who knows nobody of that name. Hero explains that it is in fact Signor Benedick of Padua to whom Beatrice refers; Beatrice then proceeds to give a damning indictment of his character. According to Beatrice, Benedick is a wastrel, a boastful flirt, conceited and empty-headed. The Messenger attempts to defend Benedick against Beatrice's onslaught, but loses miserably against her sharp wit. Leonato intercedes, explaining to the Messenger that there exists a 'kind of merry war' between Beatrice and Benedick.

Beatrice is the first to mention the idea of marriage to Benedick. Marriage to him is clearly on her mind.

The victors arrive and are warmly welcomed by Leonato. Beatrice and Benedick engage in the first of their many 'word play wars' with each other (displaying the similarities between them and the connection of minds from the start). Claudio confides to Benedick that he is in love with Hero. He questions Benedick about her but Benedick replies frivolously, claiming that he has no interest in romantic love. When Don Pedro

Benedick's response shows his distaste for romance.

is told by Benedick of Claudio's plight, he promises to woo Hero for Claudio.

COMMENT   In the nature of a true Shakespearian **comedy** (see Literary Terms), the weighty, political business is only referred to rather than being a concern of the main action. Thus the inhabitants of Messina are not touched by anything to do with the war. The victors are congratulated, and the honourable conduct of Claudio and Benedick in battle is seen as highly admirable. It is the men's behaviour as lovers which appears far more interesting and important than their behaviour as soldiers, however.

The audience are given their foundation information in this scene.

The first scene gives a great deal of information. The romantic **plot** (see Literary Terms) of Hero and Claudio is begun. The intriguing relationship between Beatrice and Benedick is an instant focus. Don John makes his presence as a shadowy figure felt more by his lack of words than anything particular he says or does.

Notice how it is Beatrice who brings up the subject of Benedick. She appears to loathe and despise him; certainly the messenger is confused by her apparent hatred of a man he has great respect for. Beatrice focuses upon attacking Benedick's behaviour towards women. Consider whether there is any substance for this condemnation. Her negative feelings seem suspiciously powerful, and Leonato's description of the 'merry war' does not completely fit with the animosity we see.

Notice how Claudio does not speak until everyone else has left the stage. It is likely that he would have been focusing his attention upon Hero whilst the others are delivering their lines.

Don Pedro's promise to 'woo' Hero for Claudio would have been accepted as normal behaviour in **courtly love** (see Literary Terms) at that time; the audience would have seen nothing unusual in it. Marriage was as much a business as a love contract; Leonato and Don Pedro appear to be very much in charge of ensuring its satisfactory conclusion. Hero is a valuable commodity: her father is wealthy and powerful and she would receive a good dowry. The final arrangements between Don Pedro and Claudio are conducted in **blank verse** which contrasts with the **prose** (see Literary Terms) of the rest of the scene. This marks the importance of their discussion.

The idea of disguise, masks and dressing up is an important **theme** (see Literary Terms) of the play. The confusion of mistaken identity arising from disguise was a common idea in the comedies.

GLOSSARY

6 **action** battle

7 **none of name** nobody important, or no 'gentlemen'

28 **Signor Mountanto** Sir Stuck Up

67 **the gentleman is not in your books** in your favour, like the phrase 'keep in your good books'

80 **run mad** fall in love

208 **heretic** traitor

SCENE 2

The discussion between Don Pedro and Claudio is mistakenly overheard by a servant. Later Leonato is

THE WOOING OF HERO continued

Antonio is eager to believe the report which we already know is false. told by his brother Antonio that it is Don Pedro who means to marry Hero. Of course Leonato is honoured and delighted. He plans to speak to Hero about it straight away in order that she be prepared to give an answer when the Prince does approach her.

COMMENT The first of the several misunderstandings takes place in this scene. This one is very short lived and inconsequential, and serves merely to set up the **theme** (see Literary Terms) of confusion and mistake in the minds of the audience. Shakespearian comedies usually involved misunderstandings, confusion and mistaken identity.

Leonato is rightly honoured that Prince Don Pedro would consider his daughter as a marriage partner. Notice how the idea of love takes second place to the tone of business arrangement. Leonato takes the news as a personal honour, and instigates and organises with a businesslike air.

Antonio is mistaken in his information. Most characters in the play are fooled by accident or plan at some point. Antonio's age does not automatically give him more wisdom or insight than the younger characters.

GLOSSARY
1 **cousin** family member
4 **strange** surprising
6 **stamps** confirms
10 **discovered** confessed
13 **instantly break with you** discuss, ask parental permission

SCENE 3
Don John is totally honest and clearsighted about his own personality. Don John and Conrade discuss the former's gloomy state of mind. It transpires that Don John is content to be no more than what he is; he refuses to manufacture any outward show of emotion. His character is clearly demarcated as an uncomplicated **malcontent** (see

Literary Terms), who needs no justification for doing
harm to others.

The same discussion between Don Pedro and Claudio
has also been overheard by Borachio, another
companion of Don John: this time the accurate state of
affairs. Borachio has just attended the formal
Think why Don welcoming supper. Don John immediately plots to
John is not in a subvert Claudio's dreams of happiness. He claims
hurry to attend himself to be 'an honest villain' who is jealous of
this formal Claudio's status and achievements. Borachio and
gathering. Conrade vow to assist him in his plans to cause trouble.

COMMENT   Shakespeare's great 'villains' tended to be uncomplicated
fellows, who did not merit any lengthy character
analysis. This scene tells us all we need to know about
Don John: that he will make mischief where he can
because that is his nature.

The Elizabethan audience would expect some mischief
from a 'bastard' brother. The status of illegitimate sons
was very low; it was deemed to be socially and morally
unacceptable to be born 'out of wedlock'. Thus
illegitimate sons were denied the same rights and
privileges under law as their legitimate siblings.
Shakespeare deliberately made Don John a 'bastard' to
mark him out as different, on the fringes of the society
he inhabits rather than a rightful member. He is
tolerated by the grace of his brother and Leonato, not
because he has the deserved honour and status of the
other men.

Don John's function in the comedy is to cause the rift,
or confusion that is a necessary part of comedy formula
(see Commentary, on Structure).

GLOSSARY   20 **stood out against** rebelled against. This speech of
Conrade's implies that Don Pedro has recently defeated
Don John's attempt to usurp his authority in some way

30 **muzzle ... clog** implying that he is restricted from free
expression

52 **forward March-chick** a negative comment, implying that
Hero is precocious

60–1 **prove food to my displeasure** give nourishment to my need
to cause misery

65–6 **their cheer is the greater that I am subdued** hinting that he
can cause trouble and so break the merriment of the
others

66 **Would the cook were o' my mind** does he mean that he
wishes the cook to poison the food?

A ⋮ *Identify the speaker.*

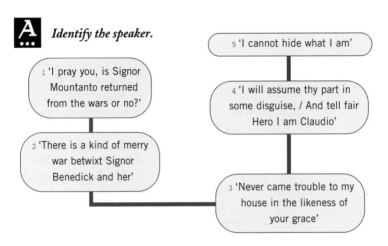

1 'I pray you, is Signor Mountanto returned from the wars or no?'

2 'There is a kind of merry war betwixt Signor Benedick and her'

3 'Never came trouble to my house in the likeness of your grace'

4 'I will assume thy part in some disguise, / And tell fair Hero I am Claudio'

5 'I cannot hide what I am'

Identify the person 'to whom' this comment refers.

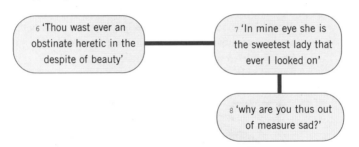

6 'Thou wast ever an obstinate heretic in the despite of beauty'

7 'In mine eye she is the sweetest lady that ever I looked on'

8 'why are you thus out of measure sad?'

Check your answers on page 78.

B ⋮ *Consider these issues.*

a Claudio and Hero are silent in the face of a large gathering. Consider how their behaviour towards each other might manifest itself on stage in Scene 1.

b Don John attests to being a man of few words in a society where expansive expression appears more customary. This places him as an outsider from the start.

c Beatrice appears to have a real loathing for Benedick, which is not taken seriously by Leonato.

d Don John is extremely envious of Claudio's status with Don Pedro.

ACT II

SCENE 1

According to the discussion which takes place now, Don John never in fact reached the supper. Beatrice, Hero and Leonato discuss what a discontented specimen he is. Once again, Beatrice wastes no time in bringing up the subject of Benedick: again to criticise him. Attention focuses upon her antipathy towards marriage, and men as marriageable propositions. She clearly enjoys the company of men, but as 'kinsmen' and friends rather than lovers. Her determination to live unmarried is a source of amusement to her companions; she wittily denounces the attractions of romantic love and men as prospective marriage partners.

Leonato reminds Hero of their previous conversation concerning preparation for a proposal from Don Pedro. Beatrice remarks that Hero needs to do as her father wishes, whereas she is in the luxurious position of being able to please herself where her future is concerned.

The theme of disguise and mistaken identity is given prominence. The 'revellers' enter: the men, all in 'masqued' disguise. The characters separate into pairs, and several discreet conversations ensue. The first is between Don Pedro and Hero; he takes her aside to 'speak of love', presumably to discuss with her the idea of marriage to

Consider whether Claudio. Next come two light-hearted, 'flirty'
Beatrice knows exchanges, the first between Margaret and Borachio,
whom she is the second between Ursula and Antonio. Then,
speaking to? It Beatrice and Benedick deliver another pointed
seems likely, given exchange: she, demanding to know who has slandered
that Margaret her, the inference being that the disguised Benedick has
and Ursula clearly just related to her some criticism of her character from
recognise their another source. She retaliates by berating Benedick's
masked character in much the same way. He is denied the
companions. opportunity to defend himself as he is in disguise.

The mischief-makers utilise the disguise **theme** (see
Literary Terms) by pretending to Claudio that they
think he is Benedick, and persuading him that Don
Pedro is wooing Hero for himself. This Claudio
instantly believes. Thus when Benedick comes to fetch
Claudio to give him the good news that Hero is now
his, he refuses to listen and promptly exits, leaving
Note that Benedick Benedick alone. He straight away turns to the
vows never to comments that 'my Lady Beatrice' has recently made
marry Beatrice, about him. When Don Pedro, Leonato and Hero enter
in similar fashion looking for Claudio, Benedick displays how hurt and
to her comment angry he has been made by Beatrice's criticisms of
in I.1. him.

Beatrice returns with Claudio; Benedick beats a hasty
retreat. The true state of affairs is explained to Claudio.
Now that this romance is finalised, attention turns to
Beatrice and Benedick. Don Pedro clearly has great
regard for both, and muses on what a good match they
would be for each other. He decides to enlist the help
of Leonato, Claudio and Hero to bring the two
together within a week; the time set aside for wedding
preparations.

COMMENT A masque was a common entertainment in Elizabethan
times: a version of our fancy dress party, where all
would wear masks or visors to hide their true identity.

Beatrice and Benedick do appear to be remarkably well suited, and well matched in wit and verbosity. They display similar attitudes towards romantic love. They also show an intriguing fascination with each other: they are never both on stage without some kind of intense exchange of words.

Note Beatrice's comments that Benedick 'lent' her his heart for a while, which may imply that they previously had a relationship.

Don Pedro remains the authority figure: he does not allow Claudio to choose the date of his own wedding. After satisfactorily concluding one romantic partnership, he takes control of another.

Don John's first attempt to cause trouble is unsuccessful. However, we are only in Act II, and it is normal for Act III or IV to contain the 'crisis' of the main plot (see Literary Terms). The audience will expect him to try again.

GLOSSARY

18 **curst** bad-tempered

38 **cuckold** man with an unfaithful wife

267 **blazon** description

296 **your Grace is too costly** you are too good for me. A polite refusal.

323 **Time goes on crutches** time goes slowly

SCENE 2

Consider whether Borachio is a faithful companion or a self-serving villain.

The tone of the play takes a more sinister turn here. Being foiled in his first attempt to cause havoc, Don John is even more determined to try again. Borachio comes up with a plot to convince Don Pedro and Claudio that Hero has been unfaithful. He tells Don John that he is 'in the favour' of Hero's waiting-woman Margaret, and can use her to pretend she is Hero and act out a love scene at Hero's bedroom window. All Don John needs to do is plant the seed of suspicion in the minds of Don Pedro and Claudio, and persuade them to observe what Borachio will show.

COMMENT   Again the use of disguise is of paramount importance in this scheme. However, the whole tenor now is far more serious: Borachio says that this plot will be enough to 'misuse the Prince, to vex Claudio, to undo Hero, and kill Leonato.'

There is a double-standard at work here.   A lady's honour was very highly prized. Hero would indeed be 'undone' if she was proven to have slept with anyone before her wedding. Brides were supposed to be virgins; if a woman slept with a man before marriage then she was no better than a prostitute. However, note Leonato's desperate comments to Claudio in IV.1, where it appears that if Hero had lost her virginity to Claudio then he would have been far more understanding.

Honour is again of prime importance. Note that the first part of the plot is for Don John to approach Don Pedro, not Claudio, with the story, the main apparent concern being for his honour as a gentleman in being associated with such a bad marriage.

Borachio is promised 1,000 ducats if this plot succeeds: a great deal of money. This shows how desperate Don John is to cause trouble; also that Borachio is only a faithful servant when there is reward in it for himself.

GLOSSARY   3 **cross** prevent

            23 **contaminated stale** prostitute, unclean woman

            26 **undo** ruin

            35 **cozened** deceived

                  semblance outward appearance, disguise

SCENE 3
Benedick's ironic description of Claudio is more like a description of himself?   Benedick muses entertainingly on the changes that love has made to Claudio's character. His prose **soliloquy** (see Literary Terms) bemoans the way Claudio is now interested only in fashion, sweet music and romantic speech, whereas he was once a good soldier, plain speaking and honest. Benedick vows never to become

such a 'fool' himself unless the perfect woman comes along – of whom he proceeds to give a description.

Benedick's solitary musing is very similar in content to the conversation Beatrice has with her friends in Scene 1.

Don Pedro, Claudio and Leonato enter. Benedick hides from them, presumably because he is irritated by the behaviour of 'Monsieur Love'. Whatever the reason, it works to great dramatic effect. The others know he is hiding, and are able to plant the seed of their plot very effectively. Benedick overhears them discussing how much Beatrice is in love with him; how Hero has said that she writes him love letters twenty times a night; how she weeps endlessly for love. She would rather die, they say, than confess any of this to Benedick for fear of his scornful nature. Benedick intersperses this 'secret' discussion with constant **asides** (see Literary Terms), demonstrating how he immediately believes what they say.

The three men exhibit great sympathy for her plight and comment warmly on her virtues. With a very ingenious twist, they also discuss Benedick's failings and muse on his unworthiness to be held in such high esteem by such a lady as Beatrice. Once satisfied that they have said everything necessary to ensnare him totally, they exit. Alone again, the stunned Benedick instantly resolves to requite Beatrice's love for him. Although slightly concerned at the reception his total change of heart may be given, he quickly manages to justify this with a deft, convenient commentary on how 'the world must be peopled' and 'doth not the appetite alter'?

Note Benedick's determination to misinterpret Beatrice's words.

Beatrice is sent to fetch him to dinner. Her behaviour towards him has not altered, but with his new perspective he hears an undercurrent of love in every word she utters.

COMMENT

The initial speech of Benedick is even more amusing given that very shortly he is to be completely taken in by Don Pedro's plot. There is a lovely sense of **dramatic irony** (see Literary Terms) here, as almost immediately he is made to recant every word of his condemnation of love.

Benedick looks for proof that the words of the plotters are correct. He assumes that if 'the white bearded fellow' Leonato has claimed Beatrice loves him, then it must be true. He also comments on the serious tone used by all, and that they were quoting Hero in much of what they said. Not for a minute does he suspect that all could be involved. He does appear very keen to believe rather than disbelieve. Perhaps he is secretly in love with Beatrice.

Although the majority of this scene is comic, the description of Beatrice's character is genuine. We have already witnessed Don Pedro and Leonato discussing her merits with affection. She is clearly highly regarded by all.

The image of bait and fishing is a **poetic device** (see Literary Terms) repeated often in this scene and the next.

<table>
<tr><td>GLOSSARY</td><td>12</td><td>drum and the fife military musical instruments</td></tr>
<tr><td></td><td>13</td><td>tabor and the pipe instruments associated with romance and social gatherings</td></tr>
<tr><td></td><td>55</td><td>sheep's guts used for making instrument strings</td></tr>
<tr><td></td><td>115</td><td>gull trick</td></tr>
<tr><td></td><td>138</td><td>flout scorn</td></tr>
<tr><td></td><td>145</td><td>ecstasy passionate frenzy</td></tr>
<tr><td></td><td>246</td><td>I am a Jew in other words, contemptible. Jews were seen as scourges of society in these times. See The Merchant of Venice</td></tr>
<tr><td></td><td>246–7</td><td>I will go get her picture find a portrait, presumably in miniature. Romantic lovers were wont to carry around tiny portraits of their loved ladies</td></tr>
</table>

A *Identify the speaker.*

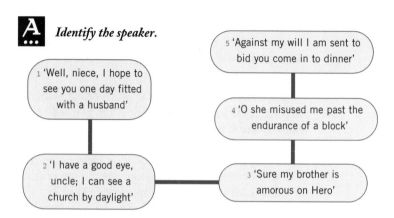

5 'Against my will I am sent to bid you come in to dinner'

1 'Well, niece, I hope to see you one day fitted with a husband'

4 'O she misused me past the endurance of a block'

2 'I have a good eye, uncle; I can see a church by daylight'

3 'Sure my brother is amorous on Hero'

Identify the person 'to whom' this comment refers.

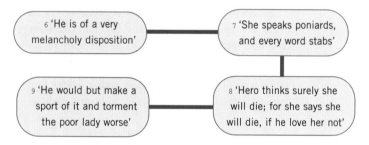

6 'He is of a very melancholy disposition'

7 'She speaks poniards, and every word stabs'

9 'He would but make a sport of it and torment the poor lady worse'

8 'Hero thinks surely she will die; for she says she will die, if he love her not'

Check your answers on page 78.

B *Consider these issues.*

a Don John refers to himself by consistent use of the pronoun 'I', which strengthens the idea of his self-absorption.

b Benedick is extremely upset by Beatrice's criticism, although he has made similar comments about her.

c Consider why Beatrice says that Benedick once had her heart.

d Don Pedro and Leonato both praise Beatrice highly, thus commending her further to the audience.

e The image of trapping, fishing and baiting continually arises in reference to being in love.

ACT III

SCENE 1 The plot to match Beatrice and Benedick is now taken over by the female characters. Hero and Ursula, after sending Margaret to fetch Beatrice, offer out a very similar kind of discussion. They sympathise with Benedick for being so in love with such a woman as Beatrice, with her hard heart making it impossible for any man, even the finest in Italy, to have their love for her returned. The scheme forms two parts: on the one hand, criticising Beatrice's scathing attitude to marriage, and on the other, praising Benedick's virtues and exhibiting great tenderness for him.

Beatrice's reaction is far more serious and heart-felt than Benedick's.

Beatrice is shocked by what she hears. Like Benedick, she instantly resolves to return his love for her, regardless of her previous attitude towards him.

COMMENT Hero is shortly to be married, therefore presumably would not share any of Beatrice's attitude towards love. It is possible that there is a thread of sincerity in her condemnation of her cousin's attitude.

The scenes are placed next to each other deliberately, making a highly charged contrast between Beatrice and Benedick's respective reactions. The first is far more humorous and **ironic** (see Literary Terms) than the second. Notice how Beatrice is silent throughout, whereas Benedick is constantly interrupting. Also, her short speech at the end of the scene is elegant **blank verse** (see Literary Terms), displaying real warmth and a desire to love and be loved in return. Benedick shows himself to be an ironic, comical character in his scene; Beatrice moves away from her previous role in hers, becoming far more serious and credible. She appears much more affected by the criticism of her character than Benedick is by what he hears of himself. It is obvious that the good opinion of her friends is very important to her.

DON JOHN'S PLOT THICKENS continued

GLOSSARY

3 **proposing** talking

12 **office** duty, function

102 **attires** outfits

106 **by haps** by chance (think of the word 'perhaps')

SCENE 2

Benedick is already demonstrating a change in personality.

The scene opens cheerfully enough, with Don Pedro, Claudio and Leonato teasing Benedick about his attitude towards love. He tries to protest but is allowed no room to speak. He finally takes Leonato to one side, presumably to discuss marriage to Beatrice.

Note Don John's formal, very courteous greeting to his brother.

The mood changes with the entrance of Don John, who tells Don Pedro and Claudio that there is great reason to suspect Hero's disloyalty. He offers them proof if they will meet him later. They resolve to do this, and Claudio furthermore swears to disgrace her publicly at the wedding if the suspicions are proved correct.

COMMENT

Don John must be aware that it is unlikely that he would be believed, for why else would he say as much to Don Pedro? Therefore, it is interesting that Don Pedro and Claudio are instantly ensnared by his words in spite of holding his character under suspicion. However implausible the accusations may appear to us, it is essential that they do believe him in order for the dramatic plot to continue.

Benedick says very little in this scene. This is an effective way of marking his change in character; once the verbose raconteur, now the subdued melancholic lover.

The **image** of fashion and dress is used in this scene to link to the **theme** (see Literary Terms) of disguise and appearance masking character.

GLOSSARY

3 **vouchsafe** permit, allow

10 **the little hangman** Cupid, god of love

31 **a Dutchman today, a Frenchman tomorrow** various fashions
of clothing

88 **holp** helped

SCENE 3

Language is a great barrier for Dogberry.

We are now introduced to the comic characters of Dogberry the constable and his assistant Verges. These two are charged with upholding law and order in Messina and are directly accountable to Leonato. Their business here is to interview the three members of the Watch, the policemen of their day. Dogberry instructs these men with their duties as watchmen, but has such confused command both of the language and his common sense that by the end of the interview it is apparent that the Watch's main function is to ignore any disturbance whatsoever.

The comic characters unwittingly enter the dramatic plot at this moment.

Luckily the Watch have slightly more instinctive common sense than Dogberry. Shortly following this interview, Conrade and Borachio enter. Borachio tells Conrade how he has just received the payment of 1,000 ducats from Don John for acting out the love scene with Margaret. According to him, Claudio and Don Pedro witnessed this as planned, and vowed to disgrace Hero publicly at the wedding. His boastful commentary is interrupted by the Watch who arrest the two men, suspecting foul play even though they clearly do not quite understand what has transpired.

COMMENT

It is customary for a scene of high dramatic tension to be closely followed by one of high comedy. The entrance of characters with a purely comic function is appropriate here. The comedy comes initially from Dogberry's hilarious attempts to speak in a high style. He uses **malapropisms** (see Literary Terms) constantly, exhibiting an inflated idea of his technical accuracy with the spoken word.

Although performing a distinct comic function, these characters also become involved in the main **plot** (see

Literary Terms) quite early in their stage life. However, in the true nature of this comedy of disguise and misunderstanding, their efforts are misunderstood even by themselves.

The acting-out part of the plot is reported rather than acted on stage. This was a common **device** (see Literary Terms) for Shakespeare to use, when it was difficult to stage a particular event.

It is interesting that law and order are upheld by such seemingly inappropriate figures. In the nature of a comedy, however, this is not so important. The state of society can never be seriously threatened with disruption, therefore there is licence to make authority figures appear unreliable. Underpinning all the comedies is a sense of security; all problems are short lived and eminently solvable.

GLOSSARY

- *9* **desartless** deserving
- *22* **senseless** sensible
- *24* **vagrom** vagrant, homeless
- *29* **knave** bad man
- *35* **tolerable** intolerable
- *91* **Vigitant** vigilant
- *124* **The vane** the weather-vane

SCENE 4

Think why Hero might have a 'heavy heart', and whether she might have misgivings about the wedding.

Hero is assisted by Margaret and Ursula to prepare for the wedding. They discuss what Hero should wear, but she finds it difficult to concentrate as she claims to have a heavy heart.

Beatrice is sent for; she shows none of her former wit, claiming to have a cold and feel too ill to get involved in her customary manner. Margaret especially teases her that she is in love.

COMMENT   Notice how Beatrice claims to feel ill, just as Benedick
           complained of a toothache in his last scene. Both are
           using physical illness to disguise the real reason for their
           dramatic change of mood.

           Once again the **theme** (see Literary Terms) of fashion
           is sharply in focus in this scene. The idea that fine
           clothes can mask true feelings highlights the idea of
           disguise running through the play.

           The women prove here to be as capable of bawdy
           humour and teasing as the men have shown themselves
           to be. There is a mood of excitement and expectation,
           which heightens the sense of **dramatic irony** (see
           Literary Terms) for the audience as they know what is
           to come.

GLOSSARY   8 **By my troth** I swear
               12 **Tire** clothing, attire
               75 **what I list** what I like
               82 **What pace is this that thy tongue keeps?** what are you
                   talking about?

SCENE 5   Dogberry and Verges report to Leonato that the Watch
           has taken two 'arrant knaves' into custody. They give no
           details as to why these men have been arrested, or

indeed who they are. Leonato is, not surprisingly, irritated by their demands that he interview them immediately, as he is on his way to the wedding of his daughter. He tells Dogberry and Verges to take the men's statement themselves, and hurries them away.

Dogberry's sense of self-importance is flattered by Leonato's instruction. It is clear that the constables still have no idea of the importance of their actions, for if they did, they would have the power to circumvent the realisation of Don John's scheme. Their report is full of the same kind of confusion and misunderstanding exhibited earlier; therefore, it is no wonder that Leonato becomes short-tempered with them.

Dramatic tension is built up by the roundabout way in which Dogberry and Verges attempt to get to the point with Leonato. The audience would feel keenly that they have the power to stop disaster if only they were more competent at their job.

There is still room for comedy, however: Dogberry shows his heightened sense of self-importance in being entrusted with the authority to interrogate the prisoners.

GLOSSARY

3 **decerns** concerns

10 **his wits are not so blunt** Dogberry means to say 'sharp'

15 **odorous** odious

17 **tedious** Dogberry interprets this as 'rich'

43 **aspicious** suspicious

47 **suffigance** Dogberry means 'sufficient'

Identify the speaker.

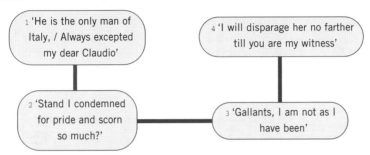

1 'He is the only man of Italy, / Always excepted my dear Claudio'

4 'I will disparage her no farther till you are my witness'

2 'Stand I condemned for pride and scorn so much?'

3 'Gallants, I am not as I have been'

Identify the person 'to whom' this comment refers.

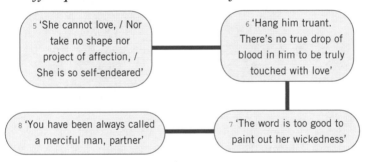

5 'She cannot love, / Nor take no shape nor project of affection, / She is so self-endeared'

6 'Hang him truant. There's no true drop of blood in him to be truly touched with love'

8 'You have been always called a merciful man, partner'

7 'The word is too good to paint out her wickedness'

Check your answers on page 78.

 Consider these issues.

a Beatrice listens carefully to the criticisms of her character and accepts them without argument. She appears as eager as Benedick to believe what she hears.

b Hero and Ursula echo the **image** (see Literary Terms) of baiting a fish used by Claudio and Don Pedro in reference to Benedick.

c Beatrice and Benedick both use the excuse of illness to disguise the reason for their subdued behaviour.

d Leonato's refusal to listen to Dogberry adds considerable dramatic tension to the scene.

ACT IV

SCENE **1**

Claudio fulfils his intention to denounce Hero as unfaithful at their wedding. In high dramatic fashion he publicly declares her to be nothing more than a whore. He claims to have proof of her infidelity. Hero's stunned reaction is taken as further proof of her guilt. All are shocked, especially Leonato who is devastated and angered beyond belief. He believes the men to be correct in their declaration however, which taxes Hero beyond her remaining strength and she faints.

Hero 'swoons' at the point where it is obvious her father also believes the lies.

Think why Don John is concerned to hurry everyone away.

Claudio, Don Pedro, their attendants and guests exit, leaving Hero, Leonato, Beatrice and Benedick with the Friar. Hero recovers from her faint and is questioned by her father. She strenuously denies the accusations. Beatrice is furiously defendant of her cousin.

The Friar steps in, coming up with a plan which could sort out the mystery. He suggests that it is widely published that Hero has died from shock. This will buy some time to ascertain the source of the slander, as well as making Claudio feel remorse for his actions. If the accusation cannot be disproved, Leonato will be able to transport Hero away secretly (presumably to a nunnery) without public notice. All agree to this plan, and the Friar attempts to comfort Hero again with the promise that the wedding is merely temporarily suspended.

All exit except Beatrice and Benedick. She is extremely upset still, and Benedick attempts to comfort her. He is impressed by the deep love and loyalty she shows for her cousin. The two openly declare their love for each other at last, and Benedick demands that she give him a task which may show how much she means to him. He is shocked by the reply: that he must 'kill Claudio'. His protestations fall on deaf ears, and he resolves to do as she requests and challenge Claudio to a duel.

Either Beatrice is making a calculated demand of Benedick, or her request is made in the heat of the moment.

COMMENT Leonato continues in the very hurried mood he exhibited in the previous scene. Notice how he commands the priest to make the ceremony very brief, cutting out everything but the bare essentials. He gives one of Claudio's answers in a most unusual manner at a wedding ceremony. This could be interpreted as the natural nervousness of a father at his daughter's wedding, or perhaps it is brought about by a sense that all is not well.

The majority of this scene is written in **blank verse** (see Literary terms) befitting the importance of its place in the drama.

Claudio's accusatory speech is full of references to disguise and masking the truth.

It is interesting to note how quickly everyone believes the slander of Hero's character, even her own father. Only the Friar, Beatrice and Benedick remain her staunch defendants. Leonato would be very concerned about his status with the other gentlemen; his place in Don Pedro's favour is very important to him. Thus he would be devastated that his daughter had done anything to lower his estimation in their eyes. It is difficult for us to have sympathy for him at this point as he so easily believes what he is told, and moreover would rather Hero die than live on with her shame. He clearly puts the word of the gentlemen above his own

*We are not meant
to judge Leonato
too harshly.*

daughter. However, it is a vital component of the dramatic turn of the **plot** (see Literary Terms) that Hero's slander is believed, therefore it does not serve to question it too closely. The audience would rest assured that everything in a comedy would have a satisfactory conclusion eventually.

Note the significantly lower status of women here. Why is it that the men are still in control of the action, and it is they who are believed rather than the women? This willingness to acknowledge a woman's lascivious nature stems from a belief that it was Eve in the Garden of Eden who caused the Fall from Grace by tempting Adam.

Margaret is a notable absentee. She is not mentioned in the stage directions. Think whether Shakespeare would have deliberately omitted her.

Beatrice and Benedick's conversation is far more serious in tone than any they have previously engaged in. Naturally this stems in part from the mood of the scene, but it also marks their new relationship with each other.

GLOSSARY

60 **Speak so wide** wide of the mark, far from the truth

142 **attired in wonder** clothed in amazement

144 **belied** lied about

183 **misprision** mistake

199 **counsel** advice

SCENE 2

*The comic subplot is
moving closer to the
dramatic action.*

In their customary bumbled fashion, Dogberry and Verges attempt to interrogate their prisoners Borachio and Conrade. They have no idea of how to go about this, or even why the men have been taken into custody. The town clerk, or Sexton, is entrusted with taking a written statement, but he has to remind Dogberry of how to conduct himself. Eventually the Watch are asked for their evidence, and Don John's

scheme is uncovered. Moreover, the Sexton reports that
Don John has fled in secret, thus proving that he has
something to hide. He manages to piece the truth
together and resolves to hurry to Leonato with the
findings.

COMMENT   This scene contains events vital to the action of the
dramatic **plot** (see Literary Terms), and yet the findings
of the court appear to take second place to the comic
value of Dogberry's misuse of language. Perhaps if more
weight were given to the drama, the tone would
become too serious for a comedy.

Don John's expedient flight is convenient. It serves as
the necessary proof of his involvement without the
potentially messy business of arrest and accusation. It
also possibly explains his desire to hurry away from the
events of the previous scene.

Pride and honour are very important to Dogberry. The
humour of his character is heightened by his need to be
taken seriously. However, the value he places upon
honour is a comic echo of the same characteristics in
the more serious characters of Don Pedro and Claudio
who value honour above all else.

GLOSSARY   _1_ **dissembly** assembly
     _3_ **malefactors** wrongdoers. Dogberry does not understand
       the term
     _5_ **exhibition** authority
   _46_ **burglary** perjury
   _69_ **suspect** respect

Identify the speaker.

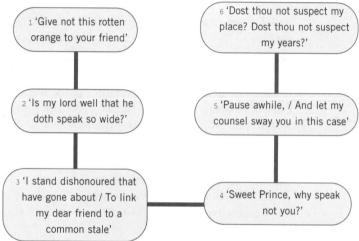

1 'Give not this rotten orange to your friend'

6 'Dost thou not suspect my place? Dost thou not suspect my years?'

2 'Is my lord well that he doth speak so wide?'

5 'Pause awhile, / And let my counsel sway you in this case'

3 'I stand dishonoured that have gone about / To link my dear friend to a common stale'

4 'Sweet Prince, why speak not you?'

Identify the person 'to whom' this comment refers.

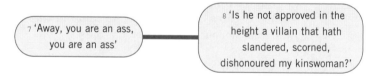

7 'Away, you are an ass, you are an ass'

8 'Is he not approved in the height a villain that hath slandered, scorned, dishonoured my kinswoman?'

Check your answers on page 78.

 Consider these issues.

a The majority of Act IV.1 is delivered in blank verse (see Literary Terms) to mark the dramatic importance of the scene.

b Benedick rightly guesses Don John to be responsible for the plot to stop the wedding.

c Hero's lack of power in this society is shown by her fainting rather than defending herself. Beatrice is much more vociferous in defence.

d Beatrice's demand that Benedick 'kill Claudio' is more desperate and demonstrative than totally serious.

A CT V

SCENE 1

*Consider why
Leonato is so
distressed.*

Antonio desperately tries to cheer his brother Leonato who has fallen into a deep depression following the recent events. Leonato refuses to be comforted, claiming that nobody can possibly understand how he feels unless they have been through a similar trauma. He vows to have the truth about Hero acknowledged, and demands that Don Pedro and Claudio be made to recognise the error of their accusation.

*Think about the
different ways of
interpreting this
part of the scene
on stage.*

Don Pedro and Claudio enter, and behave courteously towards the two older gentlemen. However, Don Pedro in particular seems loath to enter into discussion with Leonato. This suggests that either Leonato has been arguing with them previously, or that Don Pedro feels a sense of awkwardness in this delicate situation and wishes to avoid confrontation. Quarrel is not to be avoided on this occasion, as first Leonato and then the milder Antonio challenge Claudio, telling him that his 'villainous' actions have killed Hero. This Claudio and Don Pedro refuse to accept; they attempt to calm the situation down in the face of such a heated diatribe, but continue to attest to the validity of their accusations against Hero.

*Don Pedro
evidently relies
upon Benedick to
cheer him up.*

Eventually the two older brothers exit. Benedick enters, having come straight from his conference with Beatrice. He is clearly searching for Claudio. Don Pedro and Claudio greet their friend warmly. They have been looking for him in the hope that his wit and good humour will lighten their heavy hearts. They initiate the conversation, appearing to mock the actions of Leonato and Antonio; this hardly serves to endear them to either Benedick or the audience.

His part in the exchange is extremely **ironic** (see Literary Terms). They take his comments to be no more than ribaldry as is his wont; however he is serious in intent. Eventually he takes Claudio aside and privately challenges him to a duel. This is clearly not meant for Don Pedro's ears; in fact both attempt to cover up the reality of the exchange to Don Pedro.

Benedick eventually leaves, satisfied that Claudio has got the message. Before he goes he tells Don Pedro that Don John has fled Messina, that he means to fight Claudio to restore Hero's honour, and that the pair of them have 'killed a sweet and innocent lady'. He wishes to discontinue his association with all of them forthwith. Thus he leaves Don Pedro in no doubt as to his true feelings.

Still musing over Benedick's change of heart, the pair are further shocked when Dogberry, Verges and the Watch enter with their prisoners Borachio and Conrade. Borachio is made to confess all. Don Pedro and Claudio are dumbfounded, and are in the process of digesting this information when Leonato and Antonio return. Claudio immediately throws himself upon Leonato's mercy, demanding that the gentleman give him whatever penance is justifiable for the wrong he has done his daughter. Leonato asks first that Claudio spend the night at Hero's tomb and deliver an epitaph in her honour; and that the following day he marry Antonio's daughter. Claudio vows to do as he is asked.

Leonato is able to restore his dignity here.

COMMENT   When last seen, Leonato himself believed the slander against his daughter. Perhaps he has had time to reflect, or maybe the Friar has persuaded him that the rumour cannot possibly be true given his daughter's pure nature. Alternatively, maybe he was so concerned about public disgrace that he was prepared to side with the gentlemen rather than his own flesh and blood.

Given that Leonato's daughter is not, in fact, dead at all, he puts up quite a performance here. He appears to have adopted a sense of self-righteous indignation now that he has the opportunity to make Claudio suffer in return for his slanderous accusations.

It is extremely difficult to be comfortable with the attitude of Don Pedro and Claudio in this scene, particularly in their initial exchange with Benedick. Rather that feeling any sense of awkwardness, or the possibility that they have outstayed their welcome as guests of a man whose daughter they have slandered and 'killed', they merely wish to have a laugh and joke with Benedick. Of course their heartlessness towards others contrasts neatly with Benedick's honest desire to right the wrong they have done. This serves to raise his estimation greatly in the minds of the audience. No longer the cynical joker, he is now the serious gentleman on a quest to restore besmirched honour.

Remember the function of the comedy did not allow for detailed character analysis.

Claudio has lost a great deal of status during the last few scenes. In the style of romantic young lover, he has to be made to earn the worth of a good lady. In other words, it was expected that he suffer and learn a hard lesson before being fit to marry. Fairy tales and ancient myths have countless examples of the young man going away to commit some kind of difficult task before he is deemed to have earned the right to marry the beautiful princess. There is often argument about whether Claudio does show himself to be remorseful enough to deserve Hero after the atrocious way he has behaved towards her.

Leonato's request fits neatly into the **theme** (see Literary Terms) of disguise. There is no daughter of Antonio other than Beatrice, and it is not her whom Claudio is meant to marry.

GLOSSARY   *55* **beshrew** curse
                124 **scabbard** sword-case

132 **mettle** bravery

244 **Let me see his eyes** the eyes were said to be 'the windows to the soul'

269 **epitaph** poem in memory of a dead person

284 **packed in all this wrong** involved

SCENE 2

Benedick sincerely wishes to adopt the role of romantic lover, but it is far too difficult for him.

Benedick enlists the help of Margaret to write a love **sonnet** (see Literary Terms) to Beatrice. He struggles manfully for a little while, believing that in order to adopt the stance of romantic lover fully he must accord to every aspect of the stereotype. He soon concedes defeat and accepts that he must court Beatrice in his own way rather than the fashionable way.

Consider whether or not Beatrice is completely serious in her demand.

Beatrice enters and demands to know what has happened between him and Claudio. When Benedick says that they have merely had a discussion, she prepares to leave in annoyance. Benedick hurriedly explains that he has challenged Claudio to a duel; Beatrice appears satisfied with this information.

With the serious business out of the way, Benedick seems keen to return to romance. He begins to fish for compliments, asking Beatrice what first attracted her to him. She refuses to be drawn into this kind of conversation however, and very soon the pair are back to their customary baiting of each other. She mocks his need for compliments, and he defends himself by claiming that if one does not commend his own virtues then nobody else will do it for him.

Benedick returns to the more serious matter of Hero, showing great concern for her and for Beatrice. At this point Ursula enters and hurriedly explains that Don John's treachery has been discovered. The three rush off to hear more.

COMMENT

This scene contrasts sharply in tone with the previous one. It begins light-heartedly, with a return of focus upon Benedick as a comic character, struggling to adopt the stance of romantic lover. It may appear incongruous to place this scene at such a point in the drama. The function of this scene is to remind us that the play is a **romantic comedy** (see Literary Terms), and that the dramatic plot is soon to be resolved to the satisfaction of all concerned. Therefore an alleviation of the tension is appropriate at this point.

The exchange between Beatrice and Benedick in this scene is more comfortably familiar than worrying. There is none of the former bitterness in their words: the tone is one of warm and tender teasing. Given that their like-minded wit is such a connection between them, it seems logical that they use it in their romance.

Ursula has no need to go into great detail with Beatrice and Benedick, given that the audience already know all the details. The function here is to inform them so that the audience are satisfied that they know. It would be repetitive and unnecessary to give a long-winded account. Therefore her initial hurrying command serves a neat dramatic function.

The presence of Margaret is significant in this scene. Leonato left the previous scene with the intention of interviewing her to ascertain her part in the plot. Clearly all is well now, for she is in good form and functioning as a comic element.

GLOSSARY   *3* **sonnet** romantic poem, often written in praise of the virtues of a woman

29–30 **Leander ... Troilus** both romantic lovers of ancient mythology, and both subjects of romantic **epic poems** (see Literary Terms)

29–30 **not born under a rhyming planet** it is not in my nature to be able to compose verse

87 **old coil** great confusion

90 **presently** immediately

SCENE 3

Given that the scene is supposed to span a whole night, consider whether there should be a gap between Claudio's words and Don Pedro noticing that it is daylight. Think how this gap would be filled on stage.

Don Pedro and Claudio arrive at the family tomb of Leonato, where Hero's body is supposedly laid. They arrive formally, with torch-bearers and musicians. Claudio reads aloud the epitaph he has prepared in remembrance of Hero, in which he claims her wrongful accusation. He vows to return every year to perform this ceremony in honour of her memory.

Balthasar sings a song in her memory, in similar style to that of Claudio's epitaph. Then Don Pedro comments that dawn has risen, and it is time for them to return to Leonato's for the wedding of Claudio to Leonato's 'niece'.

COMMENT

The torch-bearers are there to signify nighttime. Remember that a Shakespearian theatre was unsophisticated in terms of props and lighting, and this was one way of letting the audience know the time of day. The 'vigil' the men perform customarily took place during the night.

The stage directions indicate that this scene should appear ceremonious and serious. The language is also extremely formal. Claudio and Don Pedro use rhyming **couplets** and **blank verse** rather than the **prose** (see Literary Terms) which is dominant in the rest of the play.

GLOSSARY

1 **monument** tomb. It was customary for noble families to have a family tomb where all the relatives would lie interred, similar to 'Capul's monument' in *Romeo and Juliet*

23 **rite** ritual

26 **Phoebus** in Greek mythology, Phoebus drove the carriage

that the sun-god travelled across the sky in. In other
words the sun is rising

30 **put on other weeds**   change clothes

32 **Hymen**   God of marriage

SCENE 4

*The previous
confusion is dealt
with speedily so as
to move towards
the conclusion.*

Leonato, Benedick, Antonio and the Friar discuss the
happy turn of events. The Friar reminds Leonato that
he always maintained Hero's innocence; Leonato
concedes this, adding that Don Pedro and Claudio are
likewise cleared of blame. All the fault is laid with Don
John.

Benedick comments on his relief at not having to
challenge Claudio to a duel, which adds a lighter note.
He could mean that his valour is not to be put to the
test, which would confirm his status as a comic
character; or, that he did not wish to fall out with a
friend.

Leonato instructs the ladies to hide themselves and put
on masks, and not to come until they are called.
Benedick chooses this moment (presumably because
Beatrice is out of earshot) to ask the Friar if he will
marry him and Beatrice. Leonato hints that their love is
all thanks to his assistance along with the others, but
Benedick does not understand what he means. Leonato
eventually stops teasing and merely adds his approval to
the proposed match.

Don Pedro and Claudio arrive for the 'wedding'.
Claudio reaffirms his vow to do what Leonato has
asked him, and the ladies are called for so that the
wedding proceedings may commence. Don Pedro
begins a conversation with Benedick in his customary
joking style. Again, Benedick rebuffs the attempt to be
friendly and once more begins a quarrel with Claudio.
Claudio promises to honour the challenge in time, but
their argument is interrupted by the arrival of the
disguised ladies.

Lovers are united

The disguised Hero is given to Claudio and he promises to marry her. At this point she removes her mask. Claudio and Don Pedro stand amazed that she is not dead at all; their relief is immense.

With Claudio and Hero now reunited, attention focuses upon Beatrice and Benedick. Benedick halts the Friar's wedding procession to call for Beatrice to reveal herself. The two are now in the uncomfortable position of having publicly to denounce their former shared antipathy both towards each other and to marriage in general. Benedick demands an open declaration of Beatrice's love. She is initially less brave than he and refuses to acknowledge her true feelings. As the two compare notes on what they have both heard from their friends, they appear momentarily to be slipping into their former shared aversion. This is short lived, however, as proof of each other's real feelings is provided by Claudio and Hero who present written accounts in Beatrice and Benedick's own handwriting of their love for each other. Their public kiss is final affirmation of their real affection.

Notice how Beatrice does not speak again after this kiss.

Benedick and Claudio reconcile their differences and resolve to be friends: at first apparently to keep the peace with their respective intended wives, but clearly also as they each genuinely value the other and intend to withstand each other's good-natured teasing.

News of Don John's arrest is another tidy element of the summary to this story. The final piece of news is that Don John has been captured and brought back to Messina. Don Pedro promises to deal with his brother harshly, but not until after the marriage celebrations have been completed.

COMMENT The use of disguise is once more a significant device in the play. Hero is not uncovered as herself until Claudio has proven that he will honour his promise to marry Leonato's 'niece' by taking her hand. It is only then that the real Hero reveals herself to him: to his inexpressible relief and joy and the amazed wonder of the Prince.

Don Pedro makes his second concerted effort to retrieve good relations with Benedick. He adopts their previous style of teasing conversation, presumably in an attempt to recapture their former warm friendship. It appears likely that he misses Benedick's company and humour.

Hero says very little in this scene except to show that she has forgiven Claudio. A modern audience may find this difficult to accept considering the nature of the insults thrown at her by the man she now willingly engages to marry. The conclusion is made more palatable by Claudio's deep remorse and emphatic determination to do anything to put right his wrong. Also, this is a **romantic comedy** (see Literary Terms) and as such needs to reach a tidy, satisfactory conclusion; it would not do to have the romantic heroine unhappy at the end.

Once again, Benedick displays his honesty and integrity. He uses no flowery romantic **epithets** (see Literary Terms) in his declaration; he simply and straightforwardly asks her 'dost thou not love me?' He also puts a stop to more of the same ribaldry from

Beatrice by simply kissing her. He is clearly a man of
deeds rather than words! His action here is also an
implicit comment on the misunderstandings that can
arise from over-use of language.

The news of Don John's arrest is a necessary part of the
plot; it is vital that all the loose ends are tied. The news
comes at a significant moment; the messenger enters at
the very point where both romantic partnerships are
settled. Don Pedro mirrors the tone of the play by
giving the wedding celebrations higher status than the
punishment of his brother. Nothing is to stand in the
way of the satisfactory conclusion of the romantic
festivities.

Benedick makes a significant comment on the state of
man, who he claims is 'a giddy thing': an implicit
apology for the inconsistency of human nature. The
comment draws attention to the lessons learnt by the
major characters during the course of the play, and asks
that they be allowed to learn and grow into maturity
from their errors of judgement. His words also remind
the audience that, in the manner of all theatre, 'drama
imitates life' and good drama has wider significance
than the stage in terms of human behaviour and
experience.

GLOSSARY   *17* **confirmed countenance**   straight face

                      100 **flout me**   mock me

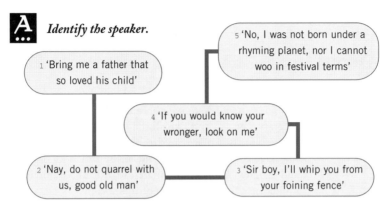

A *Identify the speaker.*

1 'Bring me a father that so loved his child'

5 'No, I was not born under a rhyming planet, nor I cannot woo in festival terms'

4 'If you would know your wronger, look on me'

2 'Nay, do not quarrel with us, good old man'

3 'Sir boy, I'll whip you from your foining fence'

Identify the person 'to whom' this comment refers.

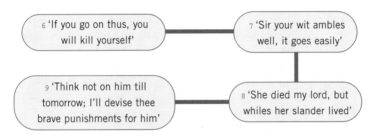

6 'If you go on thus, you will kill yourself'

7 'Sir your wit ambles well, it goes easily'

9 'Think not on him till tomorrow; I'll devise thee brave punishments for him'

8 'She died my lord, but whiles her slander lived'

Check your answers on page 78.

B *Consider these issues.*

a Leonato appears even more distressed than before. Consider whether self-righteous indignation has replaced hurt pride.

b Antonio shocks everyone by his sudden explosion of temper towards Don Pedro and Claudio.

c Don Pedro and Claudio seem uncomfortable in the presence of Leonato and Antonio.

d Benedick shows a return to his former humour in his relief at not having to fight Claudio.

e News of Don John's capture is essential to round off the play satisfactorily.

PART THREE

COMMENTARY

THEMES

LOVE

Much Ado About Nothing is a **romantic comedy** (see Literary Terms), and like all the romantic comedies its primary focus is marriage. In this microcosm of society, marriage is presented as the means by which renewal and progress are possible; therefore, it is of paramount importance to the members of this society.

Hero and Claudio present ideal marriage: young, beautiful, rich and equal.

Shakespeare offers us varying perspectives on the advisability, advantages and attractiveness of marriage through the different perspectives of the characters. Hero and Claudio are standard romantic lovers who have little to say for themselves and serve as pawns for the others to shuffle around into a satisfactory marriageable state. Their marriage is straightforward and desirable to everyone including themselves. The dramatic plot arises from a direct attempt to subvert their wedding, thereby implicitly attacking the foundations on which this society is built.

Beatrice and Benedick have similar negative attitudes to romantic love. Both characters denounce it as a viable alternative for themselves. Benedick is known to be fickle and inconsistent with women: his inability to make romantic commitments is commented on by himself and his associates. In fact, he takes pride in this facet of his character although Beatrice uses it against him on several occasions. He is attached to his self-perceived 'bachelor status' and is loath to enter the realms of romantic lover as Claudio has done: 'I will not be sworn but love may transform me to an oyster; but I'll take my oath on it, till he have made an oyster of me, he shall never make me such a fool' (II.3.21–3).

Beatrice appears to find it impossible to consider any man in the light of a possible suitor, although she complains that everyone else is getting married while she can only sit in a corner and cry 'Heigh-ho for a husband' (II.1.289). Even Hero is exasperated by Beatrice's attitude to men: 'Disdain and scorn ride sparkling in her eyes, Misprizing what they look on' (III.1.51–2). However both characters have the **convention** (see Literary Terms) of romantic comedy against them from the start. The expectation from a romantic comedy demands that the logical conclusion will be successful pairings of suitable characters. Beatrice and Benedick's posturing has immense **dramatic irony** (see Literary Terms) in the light of this convention, or assumption. Furthermore, they are paired from the start by their very similarity of nature, behaviour and attitude.

Beatrice and Benedick need to be similar so the audience can link them together.

Their joint refusal to be dewy-eyed and romantic about love presents a striking contrast to the attitudes of Claudio and Hero. There is a strong sense that Beatrice and Benedick's marriage will have an air of pragmatic realism; they already know the worst about each other before they allow themselves to fall in love. Benedick finds it impossible to play the role of **courtly** (see Literary Terms) suitor expected of him, although he struggles with poetry and fine grandiose gestures such as 'Come bid me do anything for thee' (IV.1.289). He admits his inability to fall into the role as easily as Claudio, and eventually settles for the far more realistic option: being himself. Beatrice finds it equally hard to become the 'demure heroine'; although her speech is tempered and far more serious once she has succumbed to love, she maintains her acerbic wit right up to her last words: 'I yield upon great persuasion, and partly to save your life, for I was told you were in a consumption' (V.4.94–6).

Margaret's attitude reminds us of the earthy realism of
marriage. She teases Hero on the advent of her
wedding with a reminder of the wedding night itself,
but becomes rightly critical of Hero's shocked response:
'Is there any harm in "the heavier for a husband"?
None, I think, an it be the right husband and the right
wife; otherwise 'tis light, and not heavy' (III.4.31–3).
She manages to reduce Benedick's attempt to write a
love **sonnet** (see Literary Terms) into an exchange
loaded with sexual innuendo. She refuses to
acknowledge 'courtly' expressions of love, preferring to
glory in the honest pleasure to be gained from a good
marriage.

Earthy values are
maintained:
realism matched
with idealism.

The reality of a good honest love relationship is clearly
the most desirable outcome. Courtly love conventions
are mocked from the start, and Claudio seems destined
to fail as a husband until he has become more honest
and thoughtful as a serious lover. There is always
something to laugh at in a romantic comedy; we laugh
at Claudio's innocence and Beatrice and Benedick's
protestations but are satisfied with the eventual
outcome, secure in the knowledge that the characters
have emerged into a position of deeper knowledge and
maturity.

HONOUR AND PRIDE

The value of personal pride and honour is another
important theme. All the main characters have a strong
sense of their own place in society, and their actions are
driven by a need to preserve this status. It is vital in a
comedy that order is preserved, and that any threat of
disorder be short lived and easily resolved. Thus, it is
highly significant that Don John is the one to cause
disorder, as he is the only character without real status
in that society. As an illegitimate sibling he operates

from the fringes of this world with its recognisable set
of rules and laws that govern the maintenance of a rigid
hierarchy. Elizabethans lived in a world entrenched in
the idea of order: God as the divine ruler, crown next to
God, and a rigid class system underpinning the whole
of society.

Thus each character knows his or her place, and is
fiercely defensive of it. Leonato is aware that he has
power and can choose to be a benign ruler. He expects
total compliance from Hero. His permission to marry is
sought by Claudio and Benedick. Don Pedro politely
'defers' to him, recognising that Leonato is lord of his
own house. However, Don Pedro is clearly significantly
superior to Leonato; the Prince of Arragon is senior in
status to the Governor of Messina, and Leonato is
aware of the honour landed on him if his daughter were
to marry the Prince, or even his close friend.

Status, power and wealth are very important social indicators.

When Hero's virtue is questioned, Leonato's sole
thought is for the public arena of dishonour: 'Why,
doth not every earthly thing / Cry shame upon her?'
(IV.1.118–19). His pride as a good father to a good
daughter has been damaged and this wounds him so
deeply that he wishes her dead. Don Pedro also thinks
of his own honour: 'I stand dishonoured that have gone
about / To link my dear friend to a common stale'
(IV.1.62–3). Don John cunningly uses Claudio's honour
to turn him against Hero: 'it would better fit your
honour to change your mind' (III.2.104). Both Claudio
and Benedick are similarly described as men of honour.

Pride is not to be taken too far though. Both Beatrice
and Benedick learn to temper this in themselves. Pride
is seen as a precarious thing, and they learn to shed it
when it is not serving their happiness. Pride is
commented on more humorously through Dogberry,
who has a very inflated idea of his own importance. His

pompous manner of speech and misplaced authoritative stance make him a figure of fun, purely because he does not have a shred of self-awareness about them.

APPEARANCE AND REALITY

This theme threads its way through the play on many different levels, and is highlighted by the **imagery** (see Literary Terms) of fashion, disguise and masking. Ideas about making mistakes, things not being what they seem, language confusing rather than clarifying all create a perspective of human fallibility which of course links to the overall message of the play; in Benedick's words 'Man is a giddy thing' (V.4.106), subject to inconsistency and changeability.

Think about other examples which fit this theme.

Don John 'appears' to be a loyal brother. Hero 'appears' to have been disloyal. Don Pedro and Claudio believe they have seen proof of this, but have been misled.

Claudio believes Don Pedro to be disloyal as a friend. In fact, Don John's villainy only succeeds because of the vulnerability of the other characters and the danger of trusting appearance over reality. This precariousness is highlighted in the mask scene, where the female characters all find it easy to see beyond appearance alone; and yet the drama is rooted in an inability to extend the same sense in more important matters.

Reality is manifestly in opposition to appearance in character as well as events. Beatrice and Benedick's posture is unmasked by their friends relatively easily. Claudio sheds his belief in Don Pedro's loyalty as a friend with surprising ease. Time and again outward appearances disguise reality. The characters have an inability to trust their common sense and experience, and this is made clear by Friar Francis who is the only person who pays attention to reality and appeals to the others to 'trust' his age, experience and learning.

CHARACTERS

Discussing individual characters in any Shakespearian comedy is always problematic. The characters are definite 'types' and serve distinct functions in the play. Shakespeare closely adhered to the inherent formula of the **genre** (see Literary Terms). Thus, for example, Don John's purpose and function in the plot is to provide the **crisis** (see Literary Terms), or problem, which has to be resolved in order for there to be a satisfactory conclusion. He is most definitely a one-dimensional character.

CLAUDIO

Romantic hero
Brave and
honourable
A gentleman

Claudio is the romantic hero of the play. His honour and bravery as a gentleman and soldier are made known by the messenger before his arrival on stage. He has won the regard and admiration of Don Pedro, which strengthens his position as a man worthy of respect. His love for Hero gives further testament to him being a man of good sense, and instantly wins the approval of Don Pedro, Beatrice and Leonato.

In the manner of a Shakespearian comedy, it is necessary for the romantic hero to undergo some challenge which teaches him lessons about himself and life, and from which he can emerge as a man of maturity, worthy of the love of the romantic heroine. Claudio's challenge is to be duped by his own perceived honour and status in this society. Don John manages to focus upon Claudio's most sensitive spot, which is his sense of honour. His reaction to Hero's apparently licentious behaviour centres around a sense of hurt pride and concerns about his reputation, rather than rejection by the woman he loves. His public face is very important to him.

His behaviour at the wedding can be criticised as
extremely harsh. It is important to remember that he
thinks he has proof of Hero's infidelity. He also has the
support of his friend and mentor Don Pedro, which
gives further credence to his belief. Nevertheless, it is
sometimes difficult to accept comfortably Hero's
forgiving attitude, in spite of Claudio's sincere remorse
and his vow to make recompense to Leonato. This is
where it is important to remember that in a comedy,
the satisfactory conclusion of the plot was far more
important than the inner motivations of individual
characters.

BENEDICK

Honourable and
witty
Self-aware and
cynical

Benedick's character offers a firm contrast to Claudio.
Far from being the romantic lover, he manifests
cynicism regarding all aspects of romantic love. Before
we even meet him, we hear from Beatrice that his
reputation as a scourge to all women is well known.
Although much of Beatrice's criticisms are harsh, most
of them do appear to be founded in a truth: for example
her description of him as 'the Prince's jester' (II.1.120)
which clearly wounds Benedick and does seem ratified
by the Prince's need for Benedick's 'wit'.

Benedick's behaviour is the source for much of the
comedy of the play. His elaborate posturing regarding
romance is highly **ironic** (see Literary Terms)
considering the ease with which he is ensnared into love
by Don Pedro, Claudio and Leonato. However, he is
also of equal status to Claudio in the Prince's esteem,
and has a proven record of honour and bravery in
battle. He needs to be worthy of the love of Beatrice.
He displays self-awareness and ironic self-commentary,
and learns considerable lessons throughout the course of
the play. He is the one who presents the ultimate
comment on the inconsistency of human nature,
showing how far he has travelled into a maturer
understanding of the workings of mankind.

HERO

Romantic and dutiful

Submissive and innocent

Powerless and vulnerable

The name Hero would be familiar to the Shakespearian audience: Christopher Marlowe used it for the heroine of his romantic **epic poem** (see Literary Terms) 'Hero and Leander'. Hero is synonymous with romantic heroine, therefore. Shakespeare's Hero has a straightforward role, and is one of the very few characters who does not change at all in the play: presenting a striking contrast with Beatrice especially.

Hero is a dutiful daughter. She has no independence, a fact made pointedly by Beatrice on more than one occasion. She has no autonomy within this society and moves to the will of her father, Don Pedro and Claudio. She is given no lines until Act II, strengthening the image of her as powerless. She presents the type of conventional romantic heroine, mild and meek. Her innocence is highlighted in III.4 where she is shocked by Margaret's earthy attitude to the realities of marriage. This scene focuses upon her innocence and purity, dramatically reinforcing the enormity of the accusations against her in the subsequent scene.

Hero's lack of power is further reinforced by her 'swoon' of IV.1, and again by the way others take control over the disaster and invent the death subterfuge. Even at the point of her unmasking she is acting under the direction of other characters.

BEATRICE

Independent and witty

Articulate and stubborn

Proud and loyal

Beatrice is contrasted to Hero in character as well as independence of circumstance. She is highly articulate and uses her wit constantly to attack romantic love *per se*, and especially where it pertains to herself. Therefore she is an equal match for Benedick; in fact, the two characters present male and female versions of a very similar character. Their elaborate posturing seems destined to turn itself in on them sooner or later.

Beatrice displays interest in Benedick from the start. She is the one who first mentions him, who brings him up again in a seemingly irrelevant context in II.1. She claims to abhor the idea of marriage to him, which seems odd considering he has not proposed. However, she also hints of some earlier romantic attachment between them; Don Pedro's comment that she has lost his heart meets the retort: 'Indeed my lord, he lent it me awhile, and I gave him use for it' (II.1.250). This could explain the mutual antipathy as well as the shared eagerness to requite each other's affection later on.

Although proud and stubborn, she also has a strong sense of integrity and is fiercely loyal to Hero. Hero's criticisms of her 'pride and disdain' elicit a humble sense of new-found self-awareness and desire to deserve the regard of her friends. Her 'change' is sincere and genuine.

DON PEDRO
Powerful and patriarchal

Don Pedro is the most powerful character in this mini-society, despite being a guest in Leonato's house. Leonato defers to his authority from the outset, and is overjoyed when he thinks that it is Don Pedro who wishes to marry Hero. He arrives in Messina as victor of a battle, which affirms his authority and status immediately. Clearly a gentleman and man of the world, he deals graciously with everybody, even his disloyal and treacherous brother. He controls much of the plot action of the play, being centrally involved in both romantic partnerships. He remains an isolated observer rather than integral participant however; his concern is to uphold the successful maintenance of society from a position of superior distance.

LEONATO
Benign ruler
Warm and respectful
Proud

As Governor of Messina, Leonato is a man possessed with great authority. He is benign ruler of his household, eliciting respect and warm regard from his family. He does not appear to impose his authority harshly, and appears to have relaxed ideas about status given that Margaret and Ursula are frequent participants in social situations.

Pride and honour are of great importance to him. He is flattered by Don Pedro's visit and makes great welcoming preparations. He is gracious in his speech to Don Pedro and Don John, and shows his generosity in his insistence that the party remain visitors for at least a month.

What do you think of his behaviour at the scene of the wedding?

He has a warm relationship with his family and is clearly very close to Hero, Beatrice and Antonio. He is evidently a careful father who takes his responsibilities seriously. He wishes Hero to make a good match and wants her to be prepared to think about the prospect of marriage; although he does not impose his will upon her, there is the sense that the independence he admires in Beatrice would not sit so comfortably within his own daughter.

His outburst at the wedding is irrational and extreme given what we have gathered about him before that point. He is devastated at the public disgrace and instantly blames Hero, refusing to listen to reason. His decline into absurdity is compounded by his encounter with Claudio and Don Pedro later on, where he succeeds in making himself a figure of fun in his ridiculous challenge. His credibility is restored once the truth of the plot is uncovered, and he reverts to his former ability to deal with the malefactors with reason and justice. Thus he goes through a transformation and learning process similar to that of the other major characters.

DON JOHN
An honest villain
A social pariah

Don John is a shadowy, inconsequential figure as a character; his 'type' is of more significance. He is a self-confessed uncomplicated villain, a discordant element in the play but a vital plot component. Without him there would be no story. He is evidently jealous of his

brother, there is more than one hint that the two have been enemies in the past. He is honest about himself and his rationale to hurt those around him. He is jealous of Claudio's success, and also possibly of the favour he has with Don Pedro.

Don John operates on the fringes of this society; he is there on sufferance and appears aware of this from the start. Any success he achieves is brief and short-lived, and his eventual capture and punishment a necessary part of the satisfactory conclusion.

Villains were often depicted as bastards in Shakespeare's day – to be born out of wedlock meant – in his time – that they were tainted with evil.

Dogberry

Ignorant and self-important

Dogberry's status as Town Constable would in reality be considered as important and worthy of respect. However, the state of order and justice in a comedy is never seriously threatened, which means that the authority figures can afford to be less than reliable and good at their jobs. The contrast between Dogberry's role and his fitness for duty is the major source of humour here.

The humour of his character is further compounded by his inability both to communicate clearly and to understand what is said to him. He embodies the **theme** (see Literary Terms) of language masking rather than clarifying understanding. His ludicrous self-importance seems absurd; although **ironically** (see Literary Terms) he and Verges are responsible for the successful outcome of events.

Margaret

Margaret is Hero's waiting-woman, who unwittingly becomes part of the plot to impeach Hero's character. She operates on equal terms with some of the major characters however, providing a realistic, earthy perspective on love and marriage in her conversations with Hero, Beatrice and Benedick. She has a bawdy sense of humour and is an equal match for the attentions of Borachio in II.1. She also manages to match Beatrice in terms of wit and humour, showing her to be a woman of intelligence and good humour with a down-to-earth outlook on life.

STRUCTURE

Much Ado About Nothing accords with all the **romantic comedies** in structure. The central **plot** (see Literary Terms) revolves around two pairs of young lovers. The necessary outcome of the play is marriage and celebration, but there must be a dramatic threat along the way. This threat is never allowed seriously to circumvent the happy conclusion, but is enough to disrupt drastically a smooth course of events, and potentially wreak havoc. Music and dancing play an important part in the drama as in all the comedies: music signifies celebration and merrymaking and intensifies the mood of love (II.3) and repentance (V.3). Disguise and eavesdropping are significant, sometimes more consequential than others: Don Pedro disguises himself as Claudio, Antonio's servant and Borachio eavesdrop on Claudio's confession, Beatrice and Benedick both eavesdrop on conversations about themselves and Borachio disguises Margaret as Hero.

The structure would be familiar and predictable to the audience.

The main plot focus forms two parts: Claudio and Hero on the one hand, and Beatrice and Benedick on the other. Although different in tone, both plots run concurrently towards marriage. The activity of Dogberry, Verges and the Watch only converges with the love plots in Act V, allowing a considerable amount of dramatic tension to be created along the way.

The play is written in the conventional five Acts. Acts I and II give most of the character information and allow

At the Court of Messina Sicily
A visit by Don Pedro, Prince of Arragon,
with his friends Claudio and Benedick and his
bastard brother John
to
Leonato, Governor of Messina, and
his daughter Hero (I.1)

Claudio falls for
Hero (I.1)

Beatrice and Benedick
vow never to marry (I.1)

Leonato's brother Antonio
thinks Don Pedro is in love
with Hero (I.2)

Don Pedro successfully
woos Hero...
for Claudio (II.1)

and...

decides to
engineer a romance between
Beatrice and Benedick (II.1)

Don John seeks revenge against
Claudio (I.3) and plots...

for...

Claudio and Leonato to see
Hero (actually Margaret in
disguise) flirting with Borachio
(II.2)

Benedick is tricked into thinking that
Beatrice is in love with him (II.3)
Beatrice is tricked into thinking that
Benedick is in love with her (III.1)

Don John spreads a
rumour that Hero has
been unfaithful (III.2)

Borachio's boast that he was
bribed by Don John is
overheard. He is arrested (III.3)

...

but... Dogberry fails to pass on news of the plot (III.5)

before...

The Wedding Day...

so...

Claudio denounces Hero at the altar...
and Hero faints...
and for the sake of her reputation...
she is pronounced dead (IV.1) ...

and...

Beatrice asks Benedick to duel with Claudio to prove his love
...and he agrees (IV.1)

but...

At last Hero's innocence is established (V.1)

As a consolation to Claudio, Leonato offers his niece, sight unseen, as his new bride (V.1)

Don John's trickery is revealed (V.2)

and...

after they have all prayed at Hero's tomb there is
another wedding
this time between Claudio and Leonato's niece (V.4)
All the ladies are masked
Afterwards, the bride lifts her veil to reveal... Hero

and...

Benedick and Beatrice agree to marry – on purely rational grounds...

and...

Don John is captured
After which there is general celebration

the main plots to be established. Acts III and IV move
the dramatic plot further forward, with the high drama
or 'crisis' (see Literary Terms) of IV.1. Resolving the
problem takes much of Acts IV and V, with the
restoration of order at the end.

LANGUAGE & STYLE

Shakespeare used imagery all the time. The images
were often linked to the plot and especially the theme
(see Literary Terms); in other words, there would be a
distinct set of images running through a particular play
to emphasise the mood he was trying to create in the
play. Images of fashionable dress and manners are used

*Task: make a list
of how other
clothing/fashion is
referred to.*

a great deal, particularly to make fun of characters and
criticise them: Beatrice claims that Benedick 'wears his
faith but as the fashion of his hat' (I.1.65) and Benedick
laments the way Claudio lies awake 'carving the fashion
of a new doublet' (II.3.16). Fashion and dress form a
link to the theme of appearance and reality, masking
and disguise.

Shakespeare used poetic devices (see Literary Terms)
in the language he used. The language has recognisable
hallmarks of poetry: measurable rhythm and rhyme, a
structure to each line, imagery by means of simile and
metaphor, language techniques such as alliteration and
enjambment (see Literary Terms). Elizabethan theatres
were unsophisticated places and the dramatist had to
create atmosphere, mood, plot (see Literary Terms) and
character through the power of language.

All the plays use two kinds of language: blank verse,
which is a poetic style, and prose (see Literary Terms),
which is sentences. Generally, blank verse was used
for the important, high status speeches or those of
significant characters, whereas the comic characters and

servants' speech, as well as the insignificant bits, were in prose. It was one way of indicating to the audience the significance or status of what they were hearing. *Much Ado About Nothing* uses less blank verse than many of the other plays; generally it is reserved for the 'serious' love speeches of Hero and Claudio and some of the commentary made by Leonato and Don Pedro. The significance of the prose is that it is very flexible and flowing, presumably linking to the idea of unpredictability and changeability in human nature.

Language is used to great comic effect by Dogberry and Verges. They put words in the wrong context and misunderstand the meaning of what they hear. In spite of this, language does not appear to present the problems of misinterpretation that it causes the other characters.

PART FOUR

STUDY SKILLS

HOW TO USE QUOTATIONS

One of the secrets of success in writing essays is the way you use quotations. There are five basic principles:

- Put inverted commas at the beginning and end of the quotation
- Write the quotation exactly as it appears in the original
- Do not use a quotation that repeats what you have just written
- Use the quotation so that it fits into your sentence
- Keep the quotation as short as possible

Quotations should be used to develop the line of thought in your essays.

Your comment should not duplicate what is in your quotation. For example:

Don Pedro feels that his honour has been insulted by his friend nearly marrying an immoral woman: 'I stand dishonoured that have gone about to link my friend to a common stale.'

Far more effective is to write:

Don Pedro feels insulted at the attempt to 'link my friend to a common stale'.

However, the most sophisticated way of using the writer's words is to embed them into your sentence:

Leonato's description of the 'merry war' between Beatrice and Benedick does not quite fit the reality of their behaviour towards each other.

Always lay out the lines as they appear in the text. When you use quotations in this way, you are demonstrating the ability to use text as evidence to support your ideas - not simply including words from the original to prove you have read it.

Everyone writes differently. Work through the suggestions given here and adapt the advice to suit your own style and interests. This will improve your essay-writing skills and allow your personal voice to emerge.

The following points indicate in ascending order the skills of essay writing:

- Picking out one or two facts about the story and adding the odd detail
- Writing about the text by retelling the story
- Retelling the story and adding a quotation here and there
- Organising an answer which explains what is happening in the text and giving quotations to support what you write

....

- Writing in such a way as to show that you have thought about the intentions of the writer of the text and that you understand the techniques used
- Writing at some length, giving your viewpoint on the text and commenting by picking out details to support your views
- Looking at the text as a work of art, demonstrating clear critical judgement and explaining to the reader of your essay how the enjoyment of the text is assisted by literary devices, linguistic effects and psychological insights; showing how the text relates to the time when it was written

The dotted line above represents the division between lower- and higher-level grades. Higher-level performance begins when you start to consider your response as a reader of the text. The highest level is reached when you offer an enthusiastic personal response and show how this piece of literature is a product of its time.

Coursework
essay

Set aside an hour or so at the start of your work to plan what you have to do.

- List all the points you feel are needed to cover the task. Collect page references of information and quotations that will support what you have to say. A helpful tool is the highlighter pen: this saves painstaking copying and enables you to target precisely what you want to use.

- Focus on what you consider to be the main points of the essay. Try to sum up your argument in a single sentence, which could be the closing sentence of your essay. Depending on the essay title, it could be a statement about a character: Don John is honest and open about his character; an opinion about setting: Messina is separated from the world of war, politics and money. Domestic concerns are far more important than worldly affairs in this setting; or a judgement on a theme: One of the most important themes of *Much Ado About Nothing* is romantic love and marriage.

- Make a short essay plan. Use the first paragraph to introduce the argument you wish to make. In the following paragraphs develop this argument with details, examples and other possible points of view. Sum up your argument in the last paragraph. Check you have answered the question.

- Write the essay, remembering all the time the central point you are making.

- On completion, go back over what you have written to eliminate careless errors and improve expression. Read it aloud to yourself, or, if you are feeling more confident, to a relative or friend.

If you can, try to type your essay, using a word processor. This will allow you to correct and improve your writing without spoiling its appearance.

Examination
essay

The essay written in an examination often carries more marks than the coursework essay even though it is written under considerable time pressure.

In the revision period build up notes on various aspects of the text you are using. Fortunately, in acquiring this set of York Notes on *Much Ado About Nothing*, you have made a prudent beginning! York Notes are set out to give you vital information and help you to construct your personal overview of the text.

Make notes with appropriate quotations about the key issues of the set text. Go into the examination knowing your text and having a clear set of opinions about it.

In most English Literature examinations you can take in copies of your set books. This in an enormous advantage although it may lull you into a false sense of security. Beware! There is simply not enough time in an examination to read the book from scratch.

In the
examination

- Read the question paper carefully and remind yourself what you have to do.
- Look at the questions on your set texts to select the one that most interests you and mentally work out the points you wish to stress.
- Remind yourself of the time available and how you are going to use it.
- Briefly map out a short plan in note form that will keep your writing on track and illustrate the key argument you want to make.
- Then set about writing it.
- When you have finished, check through to eliminate errors.

To summarise,
these are the
keys to success:

- **Know the text**
- **Have a clear understanding of and opinions on the storyline, characters, setting, themes and writer's concerns**
- **Select the right material**
- **Plan and write a clear response, continually bearing the question in mind**

A typical essay question on *Much Ado About Nothing* is followed by a sample essay plan in note form. This does not present the only answer to the question, merely one. Always try to use your own ideas.

Explore the theme of appearance and reality in *Much Ado About Nothing*.

Introduction

Your introduction needs to show that you understand the demands of the question by focusing on the key terms 'explore' and 'theme'. You then would briefly outline the course of your argument:

- Disguise and masking are recurrent images.
- The plot is carried forward by a series of misunderstandings.
- Most of the characters are not what they seem.
- Events are concluded with a renewed sense of reality or understanding of self and the world.

The Plot

More detailed examination of the plot is appropriate here; describe the six points of misunderstanding:

- Antonio's mistake regarding who is to marry Hero.
- Claudio believes that Don Pedro has wooed Hero for himself.
- Don Pedro and Claudio are tricked by Don John into believing they have seen Hero being unfaithful.
- Benedick is tricked into thinking Beatrice loves him.
- Beatrice is similarly tricked by Hero and Ursula.
- Claudio and Don Pedro are led to believe that Hero is dead.

Each of these devices moves the dramatic plot further forward. The main trickery caused by Don John is potentially the most damaging, whereas the other 'satellite' plots are more entertaining than seriously dramatic.

Characters

Each of the plots you have described causes change in the main characters. Describe how the following changes occur, making sure you refer to the text for examples:

- Claudio becomes more mature and firmer in his resolve.
- Benedick learns the value of love and to discard his cynical shield.
- Beatrice learns that by keeping men at a distance she has only been hurting herself.

You can also mention how the other characters learn things about themselves: for instance, Leonato believes appearance over reality until his foolish error is pointed out to him by Friar Francis. Don Pedro mistakenly trusts his brother.

Conclusion   Bringing a new idea into a conclusion works very well and leaves your reader with an extra thought. This would be a good place to mention the way language mirrors theme by making constant references to fashion, disguise and masks. Conclude by summarising what you have argued, but try not merely to reiterate everything you have said in the main body of your essay. A quotation from the play often works well as a punchy ending: 'Therefore Benedick's remark that "man is a giddy thing", is an effective closing comment from a man who has learned a great deal about human nature through the course of *Much Ado About Nothing*.'

FURTHER QUESTIONS

Make a plan as shown above and attempt these questions.

1 Compare and contrast the romance of Claudio and Hero with that of Beatrice and Benedick.
2 Describe the different types of love presented in *Much Ado About Nothing*.

3 Discuss how the character of Dogberry is linked
   to both the comic subplot and the main dramatic
   plot.
4 Describe the role of Don Pedro in the play, paying
   particular attention to what he says and how the
   other characters relate to him.
5 Leonato describes the relationship of Beatrice and
   Benedick as a 'merry war'. Discuss this description
   in the light of your own reading of the play.
6 Imagine you are to direct a production of *Much Ado
   About Nothing*. In staging Act IV, Scene 1, what
   decisions would you make regard setting, position
   of the actors and the behaviour of Claudio, Hero,
   Don John and Benedick?
7 Discuss the use of the imagery of fashion in the play
   and show it links to the theme of disguise.
8 How does Shakespeare manage to save the comedy
   of *Much Ado About Nothing* from the potentially
   tragic events of Act IV, Scene 1.
9 Why do Beatrice and Benedick get engaged to be
   married?
10 Why do you think the character of Don John is
   vital to the completeness of the play?

PART FIVE

CULTURAL CONNECTIONS

BROADER PERSPECTIVES

Shakespearian romantic comedy

Remember that *Much Ado About Nothing* is one of several in the same genre. It would be helpful to familiarise yourself with some of the others: particularly *As You Like It*, *Twelfth Night* and *A Comedy of Errors*.

Film

Kenneth Branagh's version of *Much Ado About Nothing* is a lovely film version of the play, and one which adheres strictly to the original. The film *When Harry Met Sally*, whilst not being Shakespeare, does deal with the same ideas about the problems of romantic love and compatible partners trying to get together!

The Elizabethans

Scholastic Publications publish a series of books called 'Horrible Histories', which provide accessible and entertaining information about periods in English history. *The Terrible Tudors* by Terry Deary and Neil Tongue is an easy introduction to the Elizabethan period.

Further critical reading

Dipping into works of criticism can give valuable insight into what other people say about Shakespeare's plays. Remember that you are reading opinion rather than fact though, and that your opinion is just as valid as something printed in a book of literary criticism. There are hundreds of books on Shakespeare in libraries; try Stephen and Franks, *Studying Shakespeare* (Longman: York Handbooks, 1984).

alliteration a sequence of repeated sounds in a stretch of language

aside a dramatic convention in which a character speaks in such a way that some of the characters on stage do not hear what is said, while others do. Or it may be a way for the character to convey his inner thoughts and motives direct to the audience

blank verse unrhymed iambic pentameter A common form of Elizabethan verse, closely related to patterns of speech. Used for important characters or speech in Shakespeare .

convention all forms of literature are best understood or enjoyed when the reader or audience is aware of certain common features of the particular kind of literature in question: these common features are the 'conventions' of that form

couplets, rhyming a pair of rhymed lines

courtly love stylised conventions of behaviour, adopted by fashionable men towards the women they admired. Often included serenading, writing love poetry, appearing to be miserable, etc.

crisis a vitally decisive moment in the plot of a drama

dramatic irony this occurs when the development of the plot allows the audience to possess more information about what is happening than some of the characters themselves have

enjambment a line of poetry not stopped by punctuation, allowing the meaning to carry forward into the next line

epic poem a long narrative poem in elevated style about the exploits of superhuman heroes

epithets an adjectival phrase which describes a special quality or attribute

genre the term for a kind or type of literature. The major genres of literature are poetry, drama and the novel (prose). These can be subdivided into further genres, such as narrative poetry, comedy, tragedy, autobiography, short story, science fiction, etc.

iambic pentameter a line of five iambic feet (weak stress followed by a strong stress, $-/-/-/-/-/$)

imagery using language to create a picture in the mind of the audience and thereby clarifying meaning, intensifying a mood, or adding to the theme

irony saying one thing when you mean another; in literature, irony often arises from the audience knowing more than the character

malapropism mistaken and muddled use of long words, taken from Mrs Malaprop in Sheridan's play *The Rivals*

malcontent stock character, normally the villain or outsider in a drama, who exhibits unhappiness and dissatisfaction with the world and his place in it. Often cynical

metaphor a figure of speech when two different ideas are fused together; one thing is described as being another

novella originally a short tale; nowadays used to describe a literary prose work halfway between a short story and a novel

plot basic storyline. Often a play will contain one main plot with one or more subplots running concurrently

poetic device use of stylistic techniques to achieve effects, such as alliteration, metaphor, etc.

prose sentences. Shakespeare wrote in either blank verse or prose, the prose sections normally given to the low-status characters or dialogue

romantic comedy Shakespearian romantic comedies usually centred around love, and involved stylised sets of lovers sorting out their problems satisfactorily

simile a poetic comparison, using the words 'as' or 'like' to compare one thing with another

soliloquy a dramatic speech, usually although not always in blank verse, for which the audience is the only listener. Basically a kind of 'thinking aloud', and a means by which the audience becomes privy to secret thoughts

sonnet a romantic style of poetry, fourteen lines in length

stock characters linked to conventions; stock characters exhibit familiar patterns of behaviour, such as villain, romantic hero, malcontent, servant, etc.

theme the central idea running through the piece of literature. Theme is different from plot/story in that there may be more than one theme or idea in any piece of literature

wit originally meaning 'sense' or 'intelligence', the word came to refer to the kind of poetic intelligence which combines or contrasts ideas and expressions in an unexpected and intellectually pleasing way

TEST ANSWERS

TEST YOURSELF (Act I)

A 1 Beatrice *(Scene 1)*
2 Leonato *(Scene 1)*
3 Leonato *(Scene 1)*
4 Don Pedro *(Scene 1)*
5 Don John *(Scene 3)*
6 Benedick *(Scene 1)*
7 Hero *(Scene 1)*
8 Don John *(Scene 3)*

TEST YOURSELF (Act II)

A 1 Leonato *(Scene 1)*
2 Beatrice *(Scene 1)*
3 Don John *(Scene 1)*
4 Benedick *(Scene 1)*
5 Beatrice *(Scene 3)*
6 Don John *(Scene 1)*
7 Beatrice *(Scene 1)*
8 Beatrice *(Scene 3)*
9 Benedick *(Scene 3)*

TEST YOURSELF (Act III)

A 1 Hero *(Scene 1)*
2 Beatrice *(Scene 1)*
3 Benedick *(Scene 2)*

4 Don John *(Scene 2)*
5 Beatrice *(Scene 1)*
6 Benedick *(Scene 2)*
7 Hero *(Scene 2)*
8 Dogberry *(Scene 3)*

TEST YOURSELF (Act IV)

A 1 Claudio *(Scene 1)*
2 Hero *(Scene 1)*
3 Don Pedro *(Scene 1)*
4 Leonato *(Scene 1)*
5 Friar Francis *(Scene 1)*
6 Dogberry *(Scene 2)*
7 Dogberry *(Scene 2)*
8 Claudio *(Scene 1)*

TEST YOURSELF (Act V)

A 1 Leonato *(Scene 1)*
2 Don Pedro *(Scene 1)*
3 Antonio *(Scene 1)*
4 Borachio *(Scene 1)*
5 Benedick *(Scene 2)*
6 Leonato *(Scene 1)*
7 Claudio *(Scene 1)*
8 Hero *(Scene 4)*
9 Don John *(Scene 4)*

OTHER TITLES

GCSE and equivalent levels (£3.50 each)

Maya Angelou
I Know Why the Caged Bird Sings

Jane Austen
Pride and Prejudice

Alan Ayckbourn
Absent Friends

Elizabeth Barrett Browning
Selected Poems

Robert Bolt
A Man for All Seasons

Harold Brighouse
Hobson's Choice

Charlotte Brontë
Jane Eyre

Emily Brontë
Wuthering Heights

Shelagh Delaney
A Taste of Honey

Charles Dickens
David Copperfield

Charles Dickens
Great Expectations

Charles Dickens
Hard Times

Charles Dickens
Oliver Twist

Roddy Doyle
Paddy Clarke Ha Ha Ha

George Eliot
Silas Marner

George Eliot
The Mill on the Floss

William Golding
Lord of the Flies

Oliver Goldsmith
She Stoops To Conquer

Willis Hall
The Long and the Short and the Tall

Thomas Hardy
Far from the Madding Crowd

Thomas Hardy
The Mayor of Casterbridge

Thomas Hardy
Tess of the d'Urbervilles

Thomas Hardy
The Withered Arm and other Wessex Tales

L.P. Hartley
The Go-Between

Seamus Heaney
Selected Poems

Susan Hill
I'm the King of the Castle

Barry Hines
A Kestrel for a Knave

Louise Lawrence
Children of the Dust

Harper Lee
To Kill a Mockingbird

Laurie Lee
Cider with Rosie

Arthur Miller
The Crucible

Arthur Miller
A View from the Bridge

Robert O'Brien
Z for Zachariah

Frank O'Connor
My Oedipus Complex and other stories

George Orwell
Animal Farm

J.B. Priestley
An Inspector Calls

Willy Russell
Educating Rita

Willy Russell
Our Day Out

J.D. Salinger
The Catcher in the Rye

William Shakespeare
Henry IV Part 1

William Shakespeare
Henry V

William Shakespeare
Julius Caesar

William Shakespeare
Macbeth

William Shakespeare
The Merchant of Venice

William Shakespeare
A Midsummer Night's Dream

William Shakespeare
Much Ado About Nothing

William Shakespeare
Romeo and Juliet

William Shakespeare
The Tempest

William Shakespeare
Twelfth Night

George Bernard Shaw
Pygmalion

Mary Shelley
Frankenstein

R.C. Sherriff
Journey's End

Rukshana Smith
Salt on the snow

John Steinbeck
Of Mice and Men

Robert Louis Stevenson
Dr Jekyll and Mr Hyde

Jonathan Swift
Gulliver's Travels

Robert Swindells
Daz 4 Zoe

Mildred D. Taylor
Roll of Thunder, Hear My Cry

Mark Twain
Huckleberry Finn

James Watson
Talking in Whispers

William Wordsworth
Selected Poems

A Choice of Poets

Mystery Stories of the Nineteenth Century including The Signalman

Nineteenth Century Short Stories

Poetry of the First World War

Six Women Poets

York Notes Advanced (£3.99 each)

Margaret Atwood
The Handmaid's Tale

Jane Austen
Mansfield Park

Jane Austen
Persuasion

Jane Austen
Pride and Prejudice

Alan Bennett
Talking Heads

William Blake
Songs of Innocence and of Experience

Charlotte Brontë
Jane Eyre

Emily Brontë
Wuthering Heights

Geoffrey Chaucer
The Franklin's Tale

Geoffrey Chaucer
General Prologue to the Canterbury Tales

Geoffrey Chaucer
The Wife of Bath's Prologue and Tale

Joseph Conrad
Heart of Darkness

Charles Dickens
Great Expectations

John Donne
Selected Poems

George Eliot
The Mill on the Floss

F. Scott Fitzgerald
The Great Gatsby

E.M. Forster
A Passage to India

Brian Friel
Translations

Thomas Hardy
The Mayor of Casterbridge

Thomas Hardy
Tess of the d'Urbervilles

Seamus Heaney
Selected Poems from Opened Ground

Nathaniel Hawthorne
The Scarlet Letter

James Joyce
Dubliners

John Keats
Selected Poems

Christopher Marlowe
Doctor Faustus

Arthur Miller
Death of a Salesman

Toni Morrison
Beloved

William Shakespeare
Antony and Cleopatra

William Shakespeare
As You Like It

William Shakespeare
Hamlet

William Shakespeare
King Lear

William Shakespeare
Measure for Measure

William Shakespeare
The Merchant of Venice

William Shakespeare
Much Ado About Nothing

William Shakespeare
Othello

William Shakespeare
Romeo and Juliet

William Shakespeare
The Tempest

William Shakespeare
The Winter's Tale

Mary Shelley
Frankenstein

Alice Walker
The Color Purple

Oscar Wilde
The Importance of Being Earnest

Tennessee Williams
A Streetcar Named Desire

John Webster
The Duchess of Malfi

W.B. Yeats
Selected Poems